Beagles

DOMINIQUE DE VITO

Beagles

Project Team
Editor: Heather Russell-Revesz
Copy Editor: Stephanie Fornino
Interior Design: Leah Lococo Ltd. and Stephanie Krautheim
Design Layout: Patricia Escabi

T.F.H. Publications
President/CEO: Glen S. Axelrod
Executive Vice President: Mark E. Johnson
Publisher: Christopher T. Reggio
Production Manager: Kathy Bontz

T.F.H. Publications, Inc.
One TFH Plaza
Third and Union Avenues
Neptune City, NJ 07753

Discovery Communications, Inc. Book Development Team
Marjorie Kaplan, President, Animal Planet Media
Carol LeBlanc, Vice President, Licensing
Elizabeth Bakacs, Vice President, Creative Services
Brigid Ferraro, Director, Licensing
Peggy Ang, Director, Animal Planet Marketing
Caitlin Erb, Licensing Specialist

Printed and bound in China
08 09 10 11 3 5 7 9 8 6 4 2

Library of Congress Cataloging-in-Publication Data
De Vito, Dominique
  Beagles / Dominique De Vito.
      p. cm. — (Animal planet pet care library)
  Includes index.
  ISBN 978-0-7938-3782-3 (alk. paper) 1. Beagle. I. Title.
  SF429.B3V58 2007
  636.753'7—dc22
                          2007007347

The Leader In Responsible Animal Care For Over 50 Years!®
www.tfh.com

CENTRAL
Garden & Pet

Table of Contents

Chapter 1

Why I Adore My

Beagle

What are some of the attributes of Beagles that their owners especially treasure? Beagle people gush about this breed's soulful expression, pudgy little body, saber-like tail that never stops wagging, soft ears, perfect size, desire for companionship, distinctive voice, great way with kids, happy-go-lucky attitude, independence, and cuteness!

Truth is, there are so many adjectives that fans of Beagles could use to declare why their breed is the best that summing it all up with the fact that a Beagle is a Beagle has to say it all. For Beagle owners, there is simply no other dog that can compare.

Asking people to talk about their beloved Beagle can cause them to gush with pride and love. What's amazing to think about is that the Beagle has been having this effect on people around the world for millennia.

Origins of the Beagle

Although references to Beagle-type dogs can be found in ancient Greek texts dating to 400 B.C.E., it wasn't until 1475— interestingly, the year the first book was printed in English—that we find a written reference to the modern-day Beagle: "With theyr begles in that place, And sevenscore raches at his rechase."

One thing is certain: The Beagle was developed in the United Kingdom, although his name is of international origin. It is suggested that the French word *beguele* ("open throat," or more colloquially, "loudmouth") played a part, as this could certainly describe the breed's distinctive voice. The Old English *begle* or French *beigle*, both meaning "small," also may be attributed to the Beagle's name.

The breeds that contributed to the early Beagle were thought to be the Talbot Hound and the black-and-tan Irish Kerry Beagle. The former was a white scenthound favored by William the Conqueror, who brought the breed

The Beagle was developed in the United Kingdom.

with him to the UK in the eleventh century. The latter was a small game hunter whose scenting abilities were renowned. The Beagle that evolved was a prized sportsman and companion. It is believed that Edward III, who ruled in the fourteenth century, was an avid hunter who had a pack of more than 100 Beagle hounds.

Elizabeth's Influence

Although there were certainly many in between, the next royal with a special fondness for Beagles was Queen Elizabeth I (1558–1603), the daughter of Henry VIII and Anne Boleyn. Elizabeth particularly fancied the smaller-sized or "pocket" Beagle. It was during Elizabeth's reign that Shakespeare was most prolific, the colonies were forming (Virginia was named after Elizabeth, also known as the "virgin" queen), and Beagles were sleeping in Richmond Palace.

Unlike many breeds that come to favor through an association with a celebrity and soon fall out of favor because they are more difficult to keep than expected, the Beagle's popularity only grew. As forests gave way to farmland across the UK and Europe, hounds like the Beagle were more and more prized. Foxhounds or staghounds were used by hunters on horseback, who covered many miles (km) during a hunt and who needed to be able to afford the horses to participate. Beagles, on the other hand, could be used to hunt with

Famous Beagle Owners

Probably the most famous owner of a Beagle was Charles Schultz, who immortalized his dog, Spike, in his world-famous cartoon character, Snoopy. Beagles have been the beloved companions of kings, presidents, artists, writers, sports stars, and celebrities, including: King Edward III; Queen Elizabeth I; George Washington; Grover Cleveland; Franklin D. Roosevelt; Lyndon B. Johnson; James Herriott; Stanley Coren; Chris Evert; Tom Cruise; Courtney Love; Kim Bassinger; Eva Gabor; George Hamilton; Patricia Heaton; Scott Bakkula; Travis Tritt; and of course, you!

on foot, so they weren't just for the wealthy. Although primarily a hunter of hare, Beagles also have been used to hunt small deer and fox. These hounds are very versatile—happy to work alone, in pairs, or in a pack.

The Beagle in the US

Early American settlers brought hounds and other dogs with them to assist in all aspects of establishing their new homes. These hounds needed to put food on the table, and an early favorite with the pioneers was the Black-and-Tan Hound, similar to the Kerry Beagle of Ireland. This was a larger, heavier-boned hound. The refinement of the Beagle in the US parallels the use and development of the Foxhound, a breed popularized by George Washington's passion for foxhunting.

The Beagle's size set him apart from other small-game hunters of his kind, like Foxhounds and Harriers, and it wasn't long before a smaller, closer-working hound was desirable. The true refinement of the Beagle started in earnest in the mid to late 1800s, when General Richard Rowett of Illinois led a core group of breeders to create a defining breed standard. It was Rowett and others who formed the National Beagle Club of America in 1888—two years before the formation of the Beagle Club in the UK.

In the 1940s and '50s, the popularity of the Beagle really took off in the US. There was still enough open land that sportsmen could put a small pack together and enjoy Beagling. Cottontail rabbits were plentiful, and for many, getting outdoors and hunting with their

The Beagle's size made him a popular hunting dog.

SENIOR DOG TIP
The Senior Beagle

Like people, dogs age as individuals, with some showing premature signs of aging and others not. And like people, the signs of aging in your dog are obvious and not so obvious. How comfortable your dog remains as he ages is your responsibility. Because he can't use words to tell you, you need to read his body language to determine how he's doing.

Most dogs are considered seniors when they reach the ages of 7 and older. Senior dogs slow down over time; they sleep more and have less energy and spontaneity. Beagles will show graying around their muzzles, an all-too-obvious sign of aging. You may notice that your Beagle takes more time getting up, navigating stairs, or hunting—all signs that his joints may be aching. His eyes may appear to be more sunken, and his teeth, mouth, and breath will lose the freshness of puppyhood. Your senior Beagle's "golden years" can be some of the best you share together, though, because you understand each other so well.

With your careful attention to his condition throughout his life, and working closely with your veterinarian, you will be able to give your Beagle friend the best and healthiest time with you possible.

Beagles—whether alone, in pairs, or in a pack—was an enjoyable and satisfying pastime.

The Beagle is a scenthound—he uses his nose to locate and track his quarry.

The Beagle Today

The Beagle is recognized and registered by all the world's top registries, including the American Kennel Club (AKC); the Kennel Club (UK); the United Kennel Club (UKC); the Canadian Kennel Club (CKC); the Australian National Kennel Council (ANKC); the New Zealand Kennel Club (NZKC); and the Fedération Cynologique International (FCI). Within these registries are clubs devoted to the Beagle, specifically, and to many activities in which Beagles participate, including field trials, tracking, and agility (more on what Beagles can do in Chapter 8).

The popularity of the Beagle is as strong as ever: Over the past decade, he has not fallen out of the top ten dogs registered with the AKC and has consistently been in the top five.

Physical Characteristics

For a breed to gain recognition and be able to be registered by a national or international kennel club, it must have a written standard (as well as other documentation to support its legitimacy). A breed's standard is a sort of blueprint of perfection for that breed; it's what defines the breed's characteristics and qualities so that anyone can learn what makes a Beagle a Beagle, for example, and not a breed that's similar to it, like a Harrier or Basset Hound.

The breed's standards are written by people in the countries in which they reside, so the American standard for the Beagle is slightly different from that of the New Zealand standard or the Canadian standard. The wording and focus on important attributes may be slightly different from country to country, but all clearly define the breed for its fanciers and for those around the world. It's fun to compare the standards of different countries, and by finding them online, it is much easier to do now. This discussion is based on the American standard for the Beagle.

Form and Function

The Beagle's physical characteristics stem from his purpose, which is to be a small game hunter who uses his nose to locate and track his quarry. He needs to be able to get into and through thick brush, have the stamina to hunt all day, and be able to be kept up with on foot. Obviously some important attributes would be the shape of the muzzle and head (for scenting purposes), the build of the feet and legs (durability and size), heart and lung capacity (stamina), color and coat (for visibility and protection), and of course, a voice that alerts the hunter to his location and whether he's on to something.

Size

Beagles come in two hunt-efficient sizes, or varieties: 15 inches (38 cm) tall and 13 inches (33 cm) tall. They can weigh from 18 to around 40 pounds (8 to 18 kg). The first event that featured the dogs shown in the two sizes was the Westminster Kennel Club show of 1928; it's happened that way ever since. The standard is the same for both varieties, with descriptions proportionate to the size.

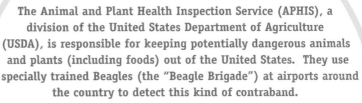

The Expert Knows

The Beagle Brigade

The Animal and Plant Health Inspection Service (APHIS), a division of the United States Department of Agriculture (USDA), is responsible for keeping potentially dangerous animals and plants (including foods) out of the United States. They use specially trained Beagles (the "Beagle Brigade") at airports around the country to detect this kind of contraband.

Why Beagles? According to APHIS, it's "because of their acute sense of smell and their gentle nature with people. Beagles' natural love of food makes them effective detectives and happy to work for treats. APHIS has found that most Beagles will remain calm in crowded, noisy locations, such as busy airport baggage claim areas. These detector dogs are bright, inquisitive, and active hounds whose superior sense of smell makes them curious wanderers by nature. Beagles have such precisely sensitive scenting ability that they can detect and identify smells so faint or diluted that even high-tech scientific equipment could not measure them."

Appearance

The breed standard carefully describes the correct appearance of a Beagle's head (skull, ears, eyes, and muzzle); body (neck, chest, shoulders, back, loin, and ribs); and running gear (forelegs, hips, thighs and hind legs, feet, coat, stern). It concludes with a General Appearance that sums up the breed and reads thusly: "A miniature Foxhound, solid and big for his inches, with the wear-and-tear look of the hound that can last in the chase and follow his quarry to the death."

Temperament and Behavior

While he can't do his job without his physical structure to support him, a Beagle is not just a Beagle for his gaily carried tail, well-muscled hips and thighs, round and firm feet, or even his soft and hound-like expression alone. He is a Beagle for these qualities and more, much more: his hunter's—and lover's—heart and soul.

Remember the way people described their Beagles at the beginning of the chapter? Some traits were related to physical attributes, but an equal number were about the Beagle's je ne sais quoi—his irresistibility factor. Soulful expression, desire for companionship, great way with kids, happy-go-lucky attitude, clowny and cuddly, and just plain cute.

These describe the Beagle's temperament and behavior.

A Happy Fellow

Beagles are amazingly even-tempered. They have gentle dispositions, and when properly socialized and cared for, get along well with other dogs, other animals, and all kinds of people—even toddlers. They love to cuddle and will want to assume their places next to you on the sofa whenever the opportunity arises. If you aren't on the sofa, no problem—they will follow you almost anywhere you go so that they can be near you. Beagles are social creatures who want to be part of the family—however large.

His Nose Knows

With so many blessings, there is one aspect of the Beagle personality that

The Beagle is a happy-go-lucky breed with a wonderful disposition.

some consider a curse (although not in the hunt field). It's his nose. The Beagle is driven by scent; it's what he's all about. No matter how much he loves you and everything you represent (cookies, soft bed, love), if he's outside and his nose locks in on something, you are a distant second on his radar. If he's not leashed and the scent is particularly intriguing, there is almost nothing you can do to stop him from giving chase. At such times he is blind to dangers like roads, other dogs, nightfall, and so on.

Three Cheers!

It may be a voice only a mother can love, so let's hope it's that way for you. The Beagle voice—it's loud, it's proud, it's persistent, it's insistent, and it's going to get your attention no matter what. Why are Beagles so vocal? They were bred and developed to alert the hunter to their location when on a scent, so whenever they detect their quarry, they are inclined to "tongue." (That's hound-speak for "bark.") To a Beagle, being happy or excited practically necessitates letting the rest of the world know. And Beagles are happy and excited a lot.

Beagles have gotten a bad reputation as nuisance barkers, and for someone who doesn't like their noise, it's understandable. Chapter 7 reviews ways to keep your Beagle's barking under control; after all, you can't take away this means of joyous expression, but you can temper it.

Beagle Central

For information on all things Beagle, visit the website of the National Beagle Club of America (NBC) at http://clubs.akc.org/NBC/. You can learn more about the history of the breed and the club, Beagle FAQs, where to find a working pack of Beagles, where to find Beagles available for rescue, and so much more. It's one to add to your list of favorite websites if you're a Beagle owner!

More for Me

Maybe another reason Beagles have withstood the tests of time is that they have a real knack for finding—and eating—food. When it comes to food, the word "fussy" is not part of the Beagle's vocabulary. What this means for you is that your pal with the most soulful of all expressions will be sitting intently by your side, his attention fully on you, while you do anything around food. His food, your food, the cat's food, the trash—it's all fair game for him! Read Chapter 3 thoroughly to learn how best to feed your forever-hungry Beagle so that he gets what he needs and not more.

Beagles and Kids

It's almost as if they were made for each other. Beagles—even puppies—get along famously with children. Children seem to warm to them, and the feeling is almost always mutual. Of course, that doesn't mean that children and Beagles can be put together anywhere at any time and all will go swimmingly. Just as with introductions between strangers, your Beagle should be properly introduced to children before being allowed to play together.

- When children want to play with your Beagle, first put them in a confined area like the kitchen or family room. You don't want them chasing the Beagle or each other all over the house.

- Children need to be told and shown how to handle the Beagle, especially a puppy. Get down on the floor with them and show them how to hold the Beagle. Explain how to pet the dog nicely, and let them know that there is to be no hitting or poking the Beagle.

- Explain that puppies can be energetic, and they explore things with their mouths (in which there are very sharp puppy teeth).

- Show the children what to do if the puppy gets overexcited around them. Rather than fussing with the puppy, they should be as still as possible, keeping their hands and feet close to their body and their face down to discourage interaction with the pup. If the puppy jumps on or bothers them, have them whimper like they're being hurt. This should startle and quiet the worked-up puppy. When he's quiet, he can be gently petted or removed from the situation.

- Have a couple of appropriate toys in the room so that the children can use them to play with the Beagle.

- Supervise the play.

The experiences that children and dogs have together shape them both for the rest of their lives. Positive experiences are wonderful; negative experiences can frighten your children and your dog, sometimes causing permanent problems. It's your responsibility to watch over the interactions to be sure that all goes well for the children and the Beagle.

A few brisk walks a day (with time to snooze, of course) should satisfy most Beagles' exercise requirements.

Energy Level

The Beagle was originally bred to spend many hours hunting over rough terrain in all kinds of weather. As Beagle owners became more pressed for time—even avid sportspeople—their hounds got out less and less regularly. This is good news for today's Beagle owners, because this development over time made the Beagle more sedentary. He's very happy in the field and will welcome any opportunity to explore the great outdoors, but he is content to snooze for many hours at a time, too. That doesn't mean that he shouldn't be exercised regularly, though.

The average Beagle is playful and energetic, and does best with at least two vigorous walks or outings a day. The vigorous part will come in between long and luxurious breaks for intense sniffing. Unless you're really pressed for time, don't deny your Beagle these sniff sessions. They are truly part of what he lives for, and he should be allowed to indulge in them. These breaks are good for you, too. Consider them "Zen moments" that you would have to pay for at a spa. Look around and let your mind wander. You'll be amazed what comes to you during these times, too.

What wonderfully happy and carefree companions are Beagles. What joy they find in coming across a strong scent. What love in their eyes when they look up to find you walking beside them. He may be a little loud, he may be stubborn at times, he may overeat, but with a Beagle, life is good.

Chapter 2

The Stuff of

Everyday Life

What's the first thing you do when you walk into your home? Do you go to the refrigerator for a drink or snack? Check the mail? Turn on the TV? Whatever it is, when you enter your space, you want to make yourself feel at home. You want to have some food in the house, and you want to be surrounded by your special things.

What does this have to do with your new Beagle? Believe it or not, he's a fellow who likes to know that when he is "home," there are special things there for him, too. He'll come to know where his food and water dishes are, where the comfiest spots are for snoozing, what the best place is for getting a glimpse or a whiff of the outside world, which doors lead to good things like food, walks, places to go potty, and so on.

Imagine how confused and even scared your Beagle will be the first day you bring him to your home. It won't be his home for him—yet—because he will not be familiar with anything in it. You can help his transition (and yours) by having what he'll need at the ready from the moment he walks in your door. If your Beagle will be joining other companion animals in your home, he will use his especially keen sense of smell to discover

where they spend their time eating, lounging, and yes, relieving themselves. That'll help him, but it may lead to possessiveness from the other members of your pack, who may see your new friend as an intruder.

So much to think about! If you plan accordingly beforehand, there will be fewer surprises for you and your friend. You'll need to gather the appropriate supplies, then think about how you want to choreograph your Beagle's first entry into your home. Involve the whole family in these exciting decisions.

Basic Supplies

When you think about having a Beagle, a relatively small and short-haired dog, you don't imagine needing too many things for his basic needs and care. But you do! There's the obvious, of course—collar, leash, food and water bowls, a brush—but you'll be surprised at how many things you'll need that you never

Whether you're bringing home a puppy or an adult, plan on purchasing supplies beforehand.

even thought about. To help, here's checklist to follow:

- baby gate(s)
- bath towels (100% cotton)
- brush
- collar
- crate
- enzymatic stain and odor cleaner
- fine-toothed comb
- first-aid kit
- food and water bowls
- food and treats
- identification tag
- leash
- license
- nail clippers
- potty pads
- shampoo
- toys
- x-pen

Collar, Leash, and ID Tag

These are certainly "must-have" items for any dog. Without them, your friend will be basically anonymous in a potentially cold, cruel world. Even the most caring rescuer will have a hard time getting your Beagle back to you if there isn't even a colored or patterned collar as an identifying accessory, much less an ID tag. And you'll certainly need a leash to walk your Beagle, or you'll be chasing after him as he gleefully hunts down whatever catches the fancy of his hunter's nose. I'm sure you get the point.

The fun thing about these items is that there are plenty to choose from. You

SENIOR DOG TIP

A New Home or an Older Beagle

If you are adopting or rescuing a Beagle, keep in mind that the poor fellow may have been through several homes before coming to yours. He will have no idea of what to expect from you, and it will be even more important that his experiences be as positive as possible from the time you acquire him. An older Beagle may have received some training, which can be helpful. Or he may have been neglected, which may make him reluctant to trust you or others in your family. Approach providing supplies for him the same way you would if you were getting a puppy. Let his start in your home be a fresh one on all fronts.

can have a lot of fun "accessorizing" your Beagle with colors, patterns, and styles. As you're considering the fashion statement you want to make, keep in mind that these are things your dog will be wearing every day and that you'll be handling quite often. For practical purposes, the first collar and leash

FAMILY-FRIENDLY TIP

Your Beagle, Your Responsibility

If deciding to bring a Beagle into your family is something you're doing for your child or children, be forewarned: Their excitement will wear off, probably sooner than you expect. The bottom line is that caring for an animal is a full-time responsibility, just as caring for a child is. A responsibility this important is not one that can be left to a child, even an older child, whose time is preoccupied with school, sports, music, friends, extracurricular activities, and so on. No matter how much your child or children will love the Beagle, he will depend on you to take care of his daily needs. A weighty job, for sure, but one that will ultimately be as rewarding as raising your children.

to have to throw away an expensive collar in a few weeks because it became too small. Wait until your youngster is full grown before exploring canine couture; the wait will give you more time to get to know your new friend, too, so you'll be able to choose things that suit his personality as well as your tastes. For example, you may want your Beagle in a collar that looks macho, like the hunter he is. But what if the camouflage patterned or orange reflector collars are too wide or clumsy looking? What if the kids are turned off by basic black? Your Beagle will be happy to help you choose the collar and leash that are best for him; most pet stores welcome dogs, so you could even try different styles before settling on something.

If your Beagle is a puppy, the ideal first collar for him is a flat buckle collar, preferably made of webbed cotton or nylon. Your puppy may have come with a collar like this. Great! Consider it a gift. These are simple to get on and off, reliable, washable, and durable.

Choosing a Leash

The ideal leash is one that's 6 feet (1.8 m) long or slightly longer. Be sure that it's washable, durable, and comfortable to hold; some nylon leashes will burn your skin if they are pulled through your hand too quickly by a lunging dog. Make sure that it's long enough to

combo you should own is one that's versatile and comfortable. If your Beagle is distracted by the feel or smell of the material—especially if he's a puppy—he may develop a habit of trying to paw at or chew the collar and/or the leash.

Choosing a Collar

Consider your Beagle's age and size when selecting a collar. You don't want

give your pal some space but not so long that the two of you get tripped up by it as you walk along.

Make sure your Beagle's collar has ID tags attached.

You'll find retractable leads among the traditional leads in any store where you shop for dog supplies. These take some getting used to and can hurt you or your Beagle if you get tangled up in the line. It's best to stick with the tried-and-true standard leash until the two of you are more familiar with each other.

ID Tag

Your Beagle's identification tag is something your pal could find distracting if it's too shiny or large. Beyond those considerations, though, tags come in an assortment of shapes and colors. An ID tag is relatively inexpensive, and if you plan to have several collars for your Beagle, be sure that each has its own tag. The personal information you should have engraved on the tag includes your dog's full name (Rover Smith, for example) and your phone numbers—home and cell if you use both frequently. Don't bother with your address. Should your dog become lost, the person who finds him will use a phone number to contact you.

Crate and Crate Supplies

We'll talk about the crate and crate training at length in Chapter 6. If you're not sure whether you should get one of these enclosures, consider the long-term expense of potentially expensive carpet-cleaning bills, damaged upholstery, chewed-up floors and cabinets, and other household damage your Beagle could do if allowed full freedom in the house. It's also helpful to have a crate-trained Beagle

Licensing Your Beagle

It's important—and easy—to get a license for your Beagle; in fact, it's the law. Simply go to your town hall and ask for a license application. Complete the questions, pay the fee, and the town will issue your dog his own license. Towns issue licenses to help them locate the owners of a stray dog and also as a health safety measure. Dogs must be vaccinated to receive a license, so it ensures that owners vaccinate their friends, especially against rabies.

when you travel so that you can crate him in the car or even on an airplane. Remember, too, that dogs are den animals. A crate is a home within a home for most dogs when used properly by you, your dog's parent.

There are several types of crates from which to choose: heavy-duty plastic ones that are often suitable for airline travel and can even be folded when not in use; folding wire mesh crates; and even soft-sided ones convenient for transporting your dog.

To help your Beagle feel at home in his crate, it should be comfy and cozy. Line the bottom with an old towel or blanket, or buy a special quilted crate pad to fit inside on the floor. If he'll be in his crate for a little while, offer him a satisfying chew toy. You may want to secure a small pail of water to the front of the crate; use something that won't spill easily.

Food and Water Bowls

Canine dishware is nearly as diverse as our own, and you can find dishes for your dog that perfectly complement your kitchen's décor. If you can find something that's safe for your dog, easy to clean, fairly resistant to breaking or knocking over, and it's a design fit, go for it. If not, cater to the practical criteria first.

Plastic may seem easy to clean and durable, but some claim that it's potentially harmful to dogs. Smell it—would you want to eat off some of the plastics being used for dog bowls? Stainless steel and crockery are safe choices. They are also both easy to clean. Be sure that any stainless steel bowls you purchase are heavy enough that they won't be easily tipped over or pushed around as your Beagle tries to

A crate is a wonderful tool for housetraining your dog.

eat out of the bowl. Think about the length of your Beagle's muzzle, too, and be sure that the bowl isn't too deep—or not deep enough. Have separate bowls for water and food.

Food: Yummy for the Tummy

We are fortunate to live in a time of continually expanding health consciousness that extends to our pets as well as to ourselves. However, just because there are more options now doesn't mean that there's any less deceptive advertising. The dog food you're drawn to in a store may appear to promise everything your Beagle needs for optimal health, but you won't know unless you take the time to really study the ingredient list, and most importantly, pay attention to how your dog looks and feels on his diet. Chapter 3 will explore in detail what you need to learn to choose foods that work best for your Beagle.

Hopefully the person or people from whom you got your Beagle told you what they were feeding him and may even have made sure that you had a few days' supply, just in case. If possible, keep feeding whatever it is he's been eating, even if you don't want to keep him on it for more than a week or so. (If that's the case, you'll want to transition foods slowly, as explained in Chapter 3.) Knowing what kind of food your Beagle has been eating, and being given at least a few meals' worth, will buy you some time in making this important decision—but not much. Your Beagle won't wait for you, and you must feed him properly from the time he comes into your care.

As for treats, the pros and cons of the various kinds available will be discussed in greater detail in Chapter 3. Suffice to say that while a treat should be a "treat," tossing your Beagle pizza crusts or other table scraps, especially sweets, could undo all the time you spend choosing

Provide your Beagle with safe, fun toys to play with.

a nutritious food. And it may lead to indigestion, flatulence, and other nasty side effects. The best treats are healthy treats.

Grooming Supplies

Your small, short-haired Beagle will be a breeze to groom, right? Compared to an Afghan Hound, absolutely. Still, you need to keep all parts of him looking good, and to do that, you'll need cotton balls, nail clippers, a toothbrush, the right kinds of brushes, and more. Learn more about which items are best for your Beagle and how to tackle the grooming routine in Chapter 4.

Toys

Shopping for doggy toys is so much fun! They come in all shapes and sizes, make funny noises, can be interactive, and much more. Before selecting what you think is cute, think about your Beagle. His desire to chew and his chewing style (mellow or aggressive or in between) will influence your choice. Some Beagles just nibble at things; some shred even the toughest materials. Leading manufacturers include safety sheets with their chews and toys to help you select appropriate toys. Follow their suggestions, and monitor your dog while he's playing. You don't want him to chew off and swallow large pieces of anything, or the squeakers that come in some toys.

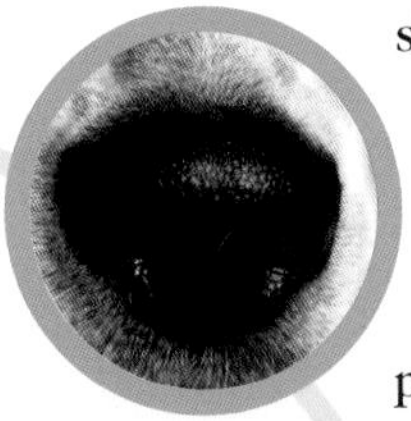

X-Pen

No, this isn't a sci-fi story about extraterrestrial Beagles wearing black. X-pen is short for exercise pen—a portable containment system for your dog. You can use an x-pen to confine your Beagle in your home the same way you would use a playpen to confine your child.

The Expert Knows

The All-Important Schedule

A crate, x-pen, or baby-gated area in your home, however safe and comfortable for your Beagle, should not be a place where you leave your dog for the day so that he won't get into trouble. Dogs are social animals, and long-term confinement and isolation will literally drive them crazy. Besides needing companionship and mental stimulation, Beagles have physical needs that must be met several times during the day—and for puppies, every few hours. That's why it's critical to establish a schedule for your Beagle. His routine must include morning and evening walks and feedings, regular breaks to go to the bathroom, and time for play and other social interactions. Your whole family should know your Beagle's schedule and be willing and able to stick to it.

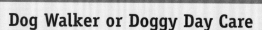

Dog Walker or Doggy Day Care

No matter how enticing or entertaining your dog's toys are, he can't be expected to amuse himself constructively with them all day, every day. He needs people and other dogs to play with. If you work all day, find someone who can provide for this need. Dog walking services and doggy day cares have sprung up across the country, and it shouldn't be difficult for you to find one or the other (or both). Your veterinarian or trainer may be able to recommend one or the other, or you can search the yellow pages or the Internet.

A dog walker is responsible for coming to your home and taking your Beagle for a walk at a designated time every day. After the walk, this person should spend some time with your dog, giving him a treat, changing his water, playing a game of tug, etc. A doggy day care center is a much more stimulating place for your Beagle, where he will be with many other dogs during his stay. The center safeguards the dogs and has a schedule for playtimes, nap times, snacks—just like a day care center for children! Whichever you choose, you will have peace of mind while you work knowing that your buddy is being taken care of.

Or you can bring one along with you on a picnic so that you know that your Beagle is safe while you relax with your family and friends. If you don't have a fenced-in yard (yet), use an x-pen at your own home to safeguard your Beagle while you are outside with the kids, gardening, etc.

Accessories

There is plenty for you to spend money on to pamper your pooch. When you're preparing for your Beagle's first few days in your home, though, think practically and don't overdo it. If you are getting a puppy, pee pee pads can help in housetraining, and you'll definitely need a pet stain and odor remover. (An enzymatic cleaner free of additional perfumes is best.) You can't go wrong with a first-aid kit. (Learn what you'll need in Chapter 5.) A baby gate (or several gates) will come in extremely handy when you want to confine your Beagle to a particular room or rooms. It's best to hold off on fun and fashionable items until you get to know your Beagle.

Chapter 3

Good Eating

True confession for Beagle owners: Beagles are the original chow hounds. Their exceptional sense of smell, hard-wired curiosity, and soulful expression give them the 1-2-3 winning combination for finding and getting food, whether it's from you or other sources (neighbors, sidewalks, small children, the cat, etc.).

The good news is that as a Beagle owner, you won't have to worry about your dog going hungry. In fact, if his appetite is ever off, you will know that a visit to the veterinarian is necessary because this doesn't happen for no reason with a Beagle. The bad news is that you must monitor and plan your Beagle's meals and food intake carefully to prevent him from overeating. You're his primary source of food, so if he feels that he isn't getting enough in his bowl during mealtimes, he's going to come looking—well, begging—for more from you at any and all opportunities. When you bring a Beagle into your home, you will always have someone watching you in the kitchen. You will be the center of unrelenting attention when you are anywhere near food. Ah, to be loved!

Beagles will eat just about anything and appear happy doing so. That doesn't make them canine garbage cans, though. There's a saying that good health starts from the inside out, and that's certainly the case with Beagles. If they eat junk, they'll look, smell, and feel bad. If they eat a nutritionally sound diet, their coats will shine, their eyes will sparkle, and their energy level will be normal. Regular grooming, adequate exercise, and mental and emotional stimulation round out what's needed for overall good health, but diet is certainly a keystone.

Another consideration is the age of your Beagle. Puppies are fed differently than adult dogs. Seniors have special dietary needs, as do dogs with food allergies or other sensitivities. Beagles are also individuals, and while the information here is as specific as possible, it is still generalized to inform the widest audience. You are the one who knows your Beagle best and who is able to tell how a food is suiting him. With lots of options out there, be informed, talk to other Beagle owners, consult with your veterinarian, and feed your Beagle a diet that makes him thrive.

Feeding your Beagle a high-quality diet is essential for his health.

Quality vs. Quantity: Nutritional Value

What you want in any food is nutritional value. That means that what's in it is actually good for your Beagle and can be used by his body. With all the selections available, it may be tempting to economize, especially when you have to spend money on a slew of supplies for your new dog. However promising the descriptions on the less expensive foods or how convenient it is to buy dog food where you do other shopping, remind yourself that your pocketbook may not be taking the hit now, but it may very well be taking more of a hit later when a poor diet affects his physical or mental health.

Does that mean the most expensive or difficult-to-find food is the best for your Beagle? Not necessarily. The bottom line is that you want your Beagle to thrive—you want his coat and eyes to shine, you want him to be relatively itch-free, you want his skin to be supple, his energy level appropriate for his age, size, and breed, and so on. When you understand what goes into commercially prepared dog foods, you can understand what's going into your dog, and you can work with it.

Dogs need certain amounts of elemental nutrients like protein, carbohydrates, fats, vitamins, and minerals. Just as we have a "food pyramid" developed by the government to give us a guideline about types and quantities of foods that are best for us,

FAMILY-FRIENDLY TIP

Letting Kids Help to Feed Your Beagle

Encourage any enthusiasm on your kids' part to feed your Beagle. If you're feeding a high-quality kibble, just rinse the bowl, measure in the food, include some warm water and/or whatever selection of goodies you want to put in the food, ask your Beagle to sit, and put the bowl on the floor.

If you include some canned food, you may want to supervise when your child needs to open a new can. The can opener itself isn't usually the problem—it's the razor-sharp lid. If the lid falls on the floor and your Beagle dashes for it, he could cut himself, too.

If your kids are old enough and interested enough, feeding the dog could be part of their daily chores. If they aren't enthusiastic about this "chore," though, cross it off their list and pick another battle. Your Beagle doesn't deserve to have his favorite time of day sullied by a moody or angry youngster.

the American Association of Food Control Officials (AAFCO) is responsible for regulating the production and sale of commercial animal foods for "safe, effective, and useful feeds." The AAFCO sets nutritional standards for dog foods, and while it's reassuring to know that a dog's basic nutritional needs are purportedly being met through the foods, the standards are generalized and should be considered guidelines only.

Dry food, or kibble, is the most popular commercial diet for dogs.

Commercial Food Choices

If you decide to feed your Beagle a commercial diet, you have the choice of dry kibble, canned, or semi-moist food.

Kibble

The cooked, hardened food that comes in bags is called kibble, and it should form the greatest part of your Beagle's diet. If your breeder or veterinarian gave you good advice about a type of kibble, you should find meat listed as the first ingredient. The ingredient panel on dog food lists what's in the food by decreasing volume, so whatever appears first is what the food contains the most of. The best ingredients should be at the front of the list. Higher-quality ingredients equate to better digestibility.

You may wonder how kibble stays fresh. Most commercial manufacturers use the natural preservatives tocopherol (vitamin E) and ascorbic acid (vitamin C). Some lower-quality foods have artificial preservatives that include the controversial ethoxyquin, BHT, and BHA. Preservatives are necessary to prevent oxidation and spoilage. You can do your part by transferring the kibble to an airtight container after you open the bag and keeping the container tightly closed when not in use.

While high-quality kibble foods contain some excellent ingredients, they still are processed at very high temperatures, which can end up "cooking out" the essential nutrients. Supplementing with foods that complement the kibble has become standard practice for many dog owners.

Canned Food

This is the stuff dogs go crazy for. Wet (canned) food has much greater aroma and flavor than kibble. It's basically commercial "stew" for dogs, featuring many fine ingredients, from the more common beef and chicken to lamb, venison, ostrich, and even fish, as well as fresh veggies and other good stuff. So why not feed straight canned food to your Beagle? There are several reasons. First, the nutrients aren't as concentrated, so you'd need to feed much more canned food than kibble to satisfy your Beagle's requirements. Also, canned food is higher in calories, which can be particularly detrimental for a Beagle. In addition, canned food doesn't promote chewing, and chewing is necessary for overall oral health and hygiene. Because canned food isn't as highly digestible as kibble, what your dog gets rid of later is softer and stinkier. And then there's cost. Feeding several cans a day adds up fast! Most dog owners add a spoonful or so of canned food to their dog's kibble to make it more desirable. The dog gets the benefits of the kibble and the canned, plus the smell and taste of the canned.

Canned food starts to break down as soon as it's opened, just as human-grade

The Expert Knows

What Not to Feed Your Beagle

Beagles will eat almost anything. They'll get great enjoyment out of leftover bits from your barbeque or pancake breakfast, but try to give them the healthiest bits. Your Beagle is not a canine garbage disposal. Some leftover hamburger is fine; a burger with a thick bun slathered in mustard and pickles is not. Remove the excess and feed just the meat.

There are some foods that dogs should not be fed no matter what. These are: alcoholic beverages; avocado; chocolate (all forms); coffee (all forms); excessively fatty foods; macadamia nuts; moldy or spoiled foods; onions; onion powder; raisins and grapes; yeast dough; and products sweetened with xylitol.

canned foods do. Put a tight-fitting lid on the unused portion and store it in the refrigerator.

Semi-Moist Food

These are dog foods manufactured to resemble ground beef or other soft meats. They tend to come in convenient single-serving pouches or bags. While not having to deal with measuring kibble or scooping and smelling canned food to prepare your Beagle's dinner may seem pleasant, the quality of semi-moist foods is generally considered much lower than the other choices. To maintain their texture and shape, these foods tend to contain more preservatives and other chemicals, including dyes. Avoid them for the long-term health of your Beagle.

Noncommercial Foods

If you decide against feeding a commercial food, you can try a raw or home-cooked diet for your Beagle. Always speak to your vet before trying a new diet for your Beagle.

Raw Diet (BARF)

In getting away from overly preserved and processed foods, some dog owners have opted to feed their dogs diets built around raw foods. Certainly the fresher and better raised the food source, the higher the quality of essential nutrients it provides. Commonly known as the Bones and Raw Food (BARF) diet, its proponents cite healthier skin and coats in their dogs, increased and more focused energy, less doggy smell, and a litany of other health benefits.

Detractors of the diet cite health risks associated with raw meat and caution that the source of the meat is critical, too. Raw supermarket chicken isn't as healthy as organic or free-range chicken. And meat can't be the only ingredient in the diet.

There are many books now available on why and how to feed a raw-based diet, and you should study them to formulate something appropriate for your individual dog.

Home-Cooked Diet

On the slightly more practical side is a home-cooked diet. It's based on the concept that once upon a time

Always have clean, fresh water available to your Beagle.

Feeding Your Older Beagle

Senior Beagles need extra tender loving care, and attention to their diet is part of that. Seniors have different nutritional needs, and most high-quality commercial kibbles come in senior formulations. There are vitamins to support age-related conditions like aching joints, and you should review what your Beagle may need with your veterinarian. Extra "live" nutrients from fresher food can help to support slower digestive and immune systems, so make a point to include fresh, steamed vegetables like broccoli, spinach, and beans, as well as fresh steamed or baked meats.

An older dog's teeth and gums may be sore, causing him to eat more slowly and carefully. Think about soaking his kibble in warm water or including more canned or home-cooked foods.

Medications your senior Beagle may need can affect his appetite and his overall appearance. Ask your veterinarian what to look for when beginning any prescription, and read up on how best to support your Beagle's system while he's taking the medicine.

It's tempting to spoil your senior Beagle, thinking that his time may be limited anyway. Beware of the effect of extra pounds (kg) and the extra effort his body needs to digest overly salty or sweet foods—moderation is always best. Ask your veterinarian whenever you have questions or concerns.

the family dog got whatever was left over from the family's main meal— pieces of cooked meat, steamed vegetables, potatoes, bread, or rice all mixed together. While it would be difficult to find a dog who wouldn't devour a home-cooked meal, the truth is that a dog's nutritional requirements are different from a human's, and providing the necessary vitamins, minerals, and other nutrients can become a time-consuming guessing game. Again, you can find information about how to ensure that a home-cooked diet provides all the nutrients your dog needs, and if it's something you feel that you can provide for your dog, chances are you'll both benefit. On a more practical note, however, you might consider using a home-cooked "stew" as a flavor enhancer as some owners do with canned dog food.

When to Feed

Feeding times vary depending on your Beagle's age. A Beagle puppy who's four months (16 weeks) old or younger should be eating four small meals a day. This should be reduced to three meals by six months and two by eight months. Beagles are happiest being fed twice a day rather than once a day through the rest of their lives. With his hearty appetite, a Beagle whose entire daily ration is given to him at one meal will spend too much time thinking about where to find other sources of food. A twice-daily feeding schedule gives him something to look forward to—and sustain him—twice a day, which is better for him all around.

Feeding times should be in the morning after your Beagle's been out to relieve himself and (unless he's a puppy) in the late afternoon or early evening. While these times certainly revolve around the times you and your family may be eating, try not to make a habit of feeding your Beagle at the same time you're putting food on your own table. It's best to feed him before your family's mealtimes; that way, even if he gives you the "I'm starving over here" look, you'll know that he's been taken care of.

Remember, too, that feeding and exercise so that your Beagle can relieve himself go paw in paw. Be sure that he has relieved himself before meals, and be sure to take him out again soon after meals. Establishing this routine will benefit you and your dog because he will know what's expected of him and won't have to worry about when he might get the chance either to eat or to go potty, and it will help to prevent house soiling accidents.

Free-Feeding

Putting an entire day's worth of food into your Beagle's bowl and leaving it for him to finish "at will," which is called free-feeding, is not healthy for your Beagle. First of all, a Beagle is not a fussy dog who will nibble, walk away, and venture back when he's bored. A Beagle is most likely to consume the entire bowl, and quickly. As discussed earlier, while a daily ration is a daily ration, it's simply more enjoyable (and healthy) for your Beagle to eat at least twice a day.

The other thing about free-feeding is that it makes you less aware of your Beagle's appetite and eating pattern. A disinterest in food is usually a first sign that there may be a health problem with your dog, and if you miss it by simply filling and then leaving your dog's food bowl as you

head out the door, his illness may become worse.

If you have more than one dog, free-feeding allows the more aggressive dogs to finish their food and then scavenge in the other dogs' bowls. For all these reasons, free-feeding is simply a bad idea, and you shouldn't do it.

How Much to Feed

Whatever you do, don't look to your Beagle to tell you whether enough is enough! His answer will always be "Never! Give me more!" Even a 15-inch (38-cm) Beagle doesn't have much of a

Puppies have different nutritional requirements than adults.

Feeding Chart for an Average Beagle

	Puppies (6 Weeks-6 months)	Adolescents (6-12) months)	Active Adults (1-6 years)	Sedentary Adults (2-6 years)	Seniors (6 years and older)
Times per day	3 to 4	2	2	2	2
Amount	3/4 cup kibble 1 tablespoon canned	1 1/2 cup kibble 1 tablespoon canned	1/2 cup kibble 1 tablespoon canned	1/4 cup kibble 1 small tablespoon canned	1/4 cup kibble 1 dollop canned food
Best Food	Commercial puppy food: 90% kibble, 10% canned	Commercial maintenance food: 90% kibble, 10% canned	Commercial maintenance food: 90% kibble, 10% canned	Commercial maintenance food: 95% kibble, 5% canned	Commercial maintenance food: 90-95% kibble, 5-10% canned

frame where he can pack away the pounds (kg). Nor is it good for your Beagle (or any dog) to be overweight. The benefit of a Beagle over a human family member with an appetite is that you can control how much your Beagle eats. In fact, you have to.

It may seem like you have your Beagle on survival rations, but try to stick to the suggestions in the feeding chart. You can feed him treats and things outside of his normal feeding times, so he's not going to starve. In the long run, you are doing your Beagle a huge favor by trying to have him maintain his boyish figure.

You'll be able to tell how your Beagle is doing on his food by how well he seems overall. If his ribs are showing too much or he seems gaunt—or perhaps a move to a colder

or hotter location has increased or decreased his necessary requirements—be sure to adjust what you feed him accordingly. Any number of things can affect how well he keeps weight on or off, and by having a general sense of what he looks like in his best health, you'll be able to maintain him that way.

Obesity

If you look at older Beagles, it seems that as a breed, Beagles must have the begging thing down because so many older dogs are overweight. They have patiently waited by their owners' sides, looking up at them longingly, waiting for any crumb that might come their way. While your friend may be momentarily satisfied with that crumb, over time his body will not be well served by it. Knowing that Beagles are prone to obesity means that it's your job to resist giving him too many extra goodies and insist that he go for regular walks.

How can you tell if your Beagle has a weight problem? Stand up and have him stand beside you. Look straight down over his back. You should see some differentiation around his loins, just before his hips and tail. Where his body sticks out some around his rib cage, it should tuck in again in the space between his ribs and his hips. Now lean over and run your hand down your dog's back. Can you feel his bones? They should certainly not be sticking out, but you should be able to feel them with some pressure. Same for his ribs. If all you feel is padding, and there is no particular "tucking in" between his ribs and hips, your Beagle should probably lose some weight. Get a second opinion from your veterinarian, who also can recommend the proper steps to help your friend lose weight without compromising his health.

Table Manners

Accepting of all parts of being in your family, your Beagle will think that it's only fair for you to reserve a seat for him at your dining table. He would try not to drool if you could be sure to give him an extra helping of potatoes.

Unfortunately for him, it can't work that way. His mealtime is his mealtime, and yours should be yours.

From puppyhood, you must train your dog to avoid your table while you eat. You don't need to banish him from the room—just be sure that he isn't begging underfoot. Put a comfy bed in the room and ask him to sit or lay down in it. If necessary, attach a leash to something near the bed so

Your Beagle is the original "chow hound"—he'll eat just about anything if you let him!

Snacks, Treats, Supplements, and Bones

Snacks—can't live without 'em, and neither should your Beagle. There are so many nutritionally sound snacks available that it's easy to choose something he thinks is tasty and you know is healthy. Here are some ideas:

- Small pieces of cheese (low fat is best)
- A couple of roasted nuts
- Small pieces of grilled, baked, or steamed meat or fish (no bones, no sauces)
- Small pieces of raw carrot (preferably organic)
- Small pieces of other fruits or vegetables, including broccoli, apple, pear, steamed green beans, cauliflower, cooked potatoes
- Small pieces of whole grain breads or crackers
- Nutritious dog "cookies"

You can indulge him in something smelly that he'll go nuts for, like one of the many doggy treats that contain additives and fats. Make these indulgences few and far between, though. They may go down easy, but they may not come out so nicely! (Nor are they healthy, but dogs do love them.)

Consider some of these same food sources as excellent healthy supplements that can be added to your Beagle's meals (in moderation):

- Low-fat natural yogurt is good for your Beagle's digestive system.
- A splash of an essential fatty acid like flax oil or fish oil does wonders for his skin and coat.

- Cooked brown rice and baked or broiled lean meats are yummy and nutritious.

A favorite treat for many dogs is a good old bone. You'll find sterile bones in most pet shops, many with hollow centers that can be filled with peanut butter or soft cheese for added appeal. The important thing is to feed a bone that won't splinter. You can freeze marrow bones from the butcher's case in the supermarket before giving them to your Beagle. He could work on one of these for hours.

There are many books that can help you decide what's best for your Beagle. Talk to other Beagle owners and your veterinarian, as well.

that he can't wander far from it. Give him an appropriate chew toy so that he can occupy himself comfortably.

While you're eating, avoid making eye contact with your Beagle or otherwise soliciting his attention. If he thinks that he can get you to look at or interact with him, he will want to join you. The biggest rule *is no feeding the Beagle from the table*. That includes feeding him after getting up from and stepping away from the table. If you're near the table during a meal and you're feeding him something from your meal, you've let him know that it's possible, and he will not give up trying to convince you to do it again.

It's okay to feed your Beagle some leftovers. Be sure to bring all the dishes to the sink, select the food, and put it in his bowl or in a stuffable chew toy. You also can put it in a plastic bag and use the food as bite-sized training treats at a later time. Dogs who aren't taught to beg from the table won't try it. Dogs who've been given table scraps or who are otherwise invited to be near the table, will beg— sometimes quite rudely.

Sit for Your Supper

Mealtime is a great time to teach and reinforce manners training. When motivated by the prospect of dinner, your Beagle will be intently focused on you. If he has to do something to get his food, chances are greater he'll do it— and do it willingly.

Teach him to sit for his dinner. With the bowl in your hand, remove a piece of kibble, show it to him, and then lure him to sit by lifting the treat up and over his nose. When his bottom hits the floor, say "Good sit," and give him the piece of kibble, then his dinner. As he gets older, he'll learn that you won't put down his bowl unless he sits, and he'll start to do it automatically. Always ask, and always reward with food and praise.

Chapter 4

Looking Good

On the list of things that are easy about caring for a Beagle, grooming is right up there. His short coat and compact size make him a true brush-and-go dog. Just because it's easy doesn't mean that grooming your Beagle is something you can neglect, however.

The Benefits of Grooming

Spending time grooming your Beagle will strengthen the bond between you. Done correctly, it's enjoyable for your Beagle because it feels good to him to be gently brushed and fussed over. For you, it's a time to get a hands-on sense of your Beagle's overall health. By paying close attention to his body while you're grooming him, you may notice bumps, cuts, nicks, swellings, or anything unusual that you wouldn't notice in passing. Once aware of these things, monitor them so that you can get your Beagle to the veterinarian if it seems something serious is developing.

Following the advice in this chapter, you will be able to keep your Beagle buddy looking, smelling, and feeling his best while getting to know him better.

Beagles are meant to be petted and fussed over, and nothing pleases their admirers more than when their coat is clean and lustrous, they aren't itchy, and they don't smell.

Getting Started

When thinking about grooming your Beagle, keep in mind that there are five primary areas that need your attention:

- coat and skin
- eyes
- ears
- feet
- mouth

A grooming table can make grooming more comfortable for you.

Grooming Supplies for Your Beagle

With the following grooming supplies, you'll be in business:

- A wire "carding" brush—a brush with short wire bristles set in soft rubber
- A hound glove—a squarish grooming mitten made of rubber with short nubs on one side
- A natural-bristled, soft brush

Grooming as a Health Check

There is no better time than while you are grooming your dog to look for a host of potential problems that may be overlooked without close attention. These include external parasites like fleas, ticks, or mange; cuts and scrapes; injury to any part of the foot; lumps, bumps, or swellings of any kind; calluses on joints; redness or irritation to any soft tissue like the gums or inside of the eyelids or ears; soreness of any kind; irritation around the anus; and so on. When caught early enough, minor irritations can be kept from becoming major irritations.

Another health benefit to regular grooming is the overall feeling of well-being it'll give your dog. Using massaging brushes and keeping dirty buildup away from his eyes and ears will keep your dog feeling good all over. And when he looks and feels good, you'll be more inclined to pet and hug him. You know he likes that!

You could spend hours working on your Beagle so that he looks like he could compete at the Westminster Kennel Club show. You could trim his whiskers, bathe him with the finest shampoo, use a shine-enhancing conditioner on his coat, and make sure that every hair was in place. But if your Beagle is itching, if his fur feels dry or thin, if there's an odor coming from any part of his body, or if he lacks the gay and charming personality of a Beagle, he won't look good for long. On the other hand, if you feed your Beagle well, give him plenty of exercise and fresh air, stimulate his mind and his senses, groom him occasionally, and delight in his enthusiasm for living, you'll have a very healthy Beagle. Feeling good is a large part of looking good.

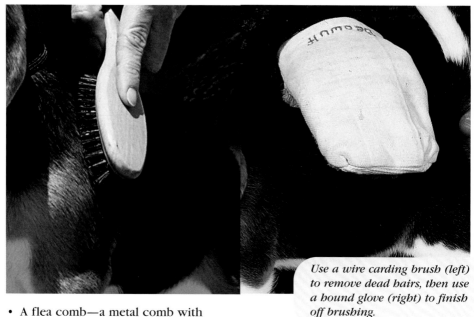

Use a wire carding brush (left) to remove dead hairs, then use a hound glove (right) to finish off brushing.

- A flea comb—a metal comb with very close tines
- Canine nail clippers—scissors or guillotine type
- Styptic powder
- Cotton balls or pads
- Canine shampoo
- Canine toothbrush and toothpaste
- Towels

Where to Groom

When it's time to groom your Beagle, find a place that's comfortable, easy to clean, and where you won't be disturbed. Because of his size, you'll need to get down to his level or bring him up to yours. If you prefer the former, get down on the floor with him and groom him in your lap with a towel under him. He will need to stand or sit while you brush his top and take care of his face and ears. He will need to lie still while you clean his tummy and legs, and take care of his feet and nails. If this sounds like it might be awkward or uncomfortable after a while, consider purchasing or creating a grooming table for your Beagle.

Using a Grooming Table

Getting down on the floor to properly groom a small dog can be hard on your joints and downright awkward. You'll have a better perspective and probably do a better job if you have your Beagle in a position where you can comfortably groom him while you're standing and moving around him. The grooming table is the ticket.

You can purchase a grooming table at a pet supply store. Lightweight yet sturdy, the table can be folded when not in use and comes with a hooked arm on which to attach a leash, as well as a padded surface for the dog to stand on. You also can try to use one of your own tables as a grooming table, although this will mean that you have to set it up, take it apart, and thoroughly clean the table whenever you convert it. All you'll need, though, is a piece of nonskid rubber large enough for your dog to move around on and to catch dead hair and dirt. You'll need to hold your Beagle's leash because you won't have a place to attach it, but once your dog gets used to the experience, you might not even need a leash.

Brushing Your Beagle

Keep your grooming tools in a large container so that they're all together when you need them. With your Beagle on a leash and either in your lap or on the table, begin brushing him with the wire carding brush. Start at his head and work back to his tail. This brush will remove dead hairs while stimulating the skin. Be sure to brush behind your Beagle's ears, along his sides, down his legs, and over his whole tail.

When you've finished with the wire brush, go over your friend again with the hound glove to loosen any stray dead hairs and to give him a nice massaging experience. Finish with the natural bristle brush to bring the coat back into position.

Cleaning Your Beagle's Eyes

When you're finished brushing, focus on your Beagle's head. Use damp cotton balls to remove any buildup around his eyes and to wipe down the hair on his face. Take a close look at his eyes as you wipe around them. They should be clear and bright, and

FAMILY-FRIENDLY TIP

What Your Kids Can Do to Help

If your kids seem interested in helping to groom your Beagle, encourage them! Before you let them loose with the brushes, though, show them how to do it and be firm about what you expect. The dog is not a stuffed animal or doll and can easily be hurt when brushed too roughly. Supervise your child the first few times she does it so that you know that she can. Don't let young children handle anything sharp or potentially harmful around the dog, like the nail clippers, scissors, toothbrush or even the wire brush. Let them do the easy body work, and do the more demanding work yourself.

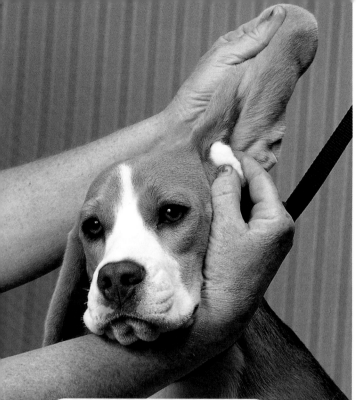

Your Beagle's droopy ears make him prone to infections—be sure to inspect them every grooming session.

should hear a squishing sound. With a cotton ball, wipe away the excess oil and debris, making sure not to insert the ball too far down into the ear. Use a cotton ball or pad to dab away at debris in the crevices of the ear, but be careful not to poke anything into the ear.

Trimming Your Beagle's Nails

When you've finished grooming the top and sides of your Beagle, move to his feet. He will need to lie down so that you can work with his paws. (Because his belly will be exposed, this is a good time to gently brush away any accumulated dirt on his stomach with the bristle brush.)

To trim the nails, take a paw in your hand and hold it near the pad so that you have control over the toe and nail. The important thing here is not to cut off too much nail, or you'll cut into the nail's nerve ending—the quick—which will hurt and bleed (sometimes profusely). Always err on the side of removing too little nail to avoid the quick. You can always trim off more in a day or so. If you do cut into the quick, use a cotton ball until the bleeding subsides somewhat, then dab styptic powder on the nail.

With the nail exposed, position the clipper so that just the tip of the nail is in it, and clip the end off. If your Beagle is sensitive, praise him for his cooperation. Consider taking breaks

the skin around them should be firm and pink inside.

Cleaning Your Beagle's Ears

After the brushing and eye check, clean your Beagle's ears. With his floppy ears, the Beagle is more prone to ear problems because the air circulation around the inner ear isn't as good. Wipe the outsides, and lift them to inspect under the ear flap. About once a month, put a drop of mineral oil into the ear and massage around the base of the ear. You

between nails and giving him a treat when he is a good boy. If he squirms too much and you feel that you can't do his nails, make an appointment to have the veterinarian clip them for you. Watching someone with experience can give you the confidence to do it yourself—or at least the assurance that the nails are being cut correctly.

Bathing Your Beagle

Here's more good news: The only time you should need to bathe your Beagle is if he has rolled in or been sprayed by something really stinky, or if he comes home from a hunt covered in mud. Truthfully, the less often you bathe your Beagle, the healthier his skin and coat will be. Even with the moisturizing shampoos and conditioners designed for dogs, your Beagle's natural oils are his best protection against dirt, odor, and irritants. Too-frequent bathing can strip the oils.

That said, there will be those times when your Beagle must have a bath, so you should know what to do. First, gather your supplies so that you have everything at hand: shampoo, a plastic container to use for rinsing, and a few clean, dry towels. If you'll be washing your Beagle in the tub or a large sink, put a rubber mat in it for traction, and keep his collar on for extra control. Unless he's caked in gunk, brush him before bathing him.

With the warm water running gently, put your dog in the tub. Begin wetting

him with water from the container—don't push him under the faucet. Speak reassuringly to him as you get him wet. Very few dogs enjoy being bathed, so expect your Beagle to struggle a bit. Once he's wet all over, apply shampoo

SENIOR DOG TIP

Grooming an Older Dog

Senior Beagles especially appreciate the attention they get from grooming, and the health benefits will really start to pay off. If you notice that your Beagle's hock seems sore while you're wiping down his legs, start to pay more attention to how he's getting up and down and moving around in general. He may need a pain reliever or joint supplement. Older dogs develop a host of lumps and bumps, including fatty tumors that should be checked by your veterinarian to be sure that they're benign. Beagles who are occasionally incontinent will benefit from "dry baths" using specially formulated odor-killing wipes so that they don't have to be taken in and out of the tub. Check your senior's eyes for any clouding or discoloration, and keep brushing those teeth and gums!

47

Looking Good

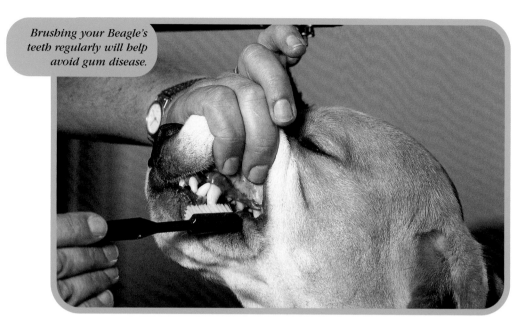

along his back from his neck down. You can wash his neck and the top of his head with the lather from his back. Don't put shampoo directly on his head or face because it will irritate his eyes and nose. Work the shampoo into a lather on his body and down his legs, being sure to get some on his tummy and between his legs, too. Don't forget to wash his tail.

When you've scrubbed him all over, begin to rinse, again applying warm water from the container, not from the faucet. Rinse thoroughly, then rinse again. You want to remove all soapy residue from the fur. Use a wet washcloth around your Beagle's face.

Drying
When he's thoroughly rinsed, turn the water off and use a thick towel to dry

him as best you can. He'll be excited to be out of the tub and finished with his bath. He may want to roll on the carpet or on your bed, or in a muddy spot if you take him outside. You may want to follow him with the towel or walk him on leash while he air-dries so that he doesn't get into too much trouble. Beagles dry fairly quickly, and you'll both be pleased with how handsome he looks. Give him a cookie for suffering through the indignity, and give yourself a cookie for doing such a good job.

Your Beagle's Teeth and Gums
If you grew up in a household with dogs, chances are your parents didn't brush your dog's teeth. It just wasn't the thing to do once upon a time. But you probably did notice how

your older dogs' breath stank or how dirty their teeth were when they panted. Oral health for dogs has come a long way in the past few decades, and dogs are definitely benefiting.

There are now many canine toothbrushes and toothpastes from which to choose, as well as products designed to help to strengthen teeth and jaws and reduce plaque and tartar buildup. Take advantage of these products!

Veterinarians recommend brushing your dog's teeth every day, just as you do your own. Realistically, if you can manage to do this for your dog even once a week, your Beagle will be in great shape.

Using the Brush and Paste

The toughest part about brushing your dog's teeth is getting both of you used to it. With flavored toothpaste, the experience isn't quite as unpleasant for your dog, but he still needs to put up with the brush being moved around his mouth. When you're starting, do only one part of the mouth at a time. Finish by giving him a hard dog cookie and a clean bowl of water for his refreshment.

To brush the teeth, just put a dab of paste on the brush, hold his head, and then part his lips so that you can position the brush on his teeth. Brush up and down and along the gum line, reaching back and doing the back teeth when your Beagle is acclimated to the procedure. Speak in a positive, reassuring voice to your Beagle while you brush so that he thinks that you think that this is the most wonderful thing. He'll soon get used to it, and your vet will be really impressed.

Chapter 5

Feeling Good

The Beagle, as a breed, is a hardy, fairly low-maintenance hound whose basic needs are fairly easily met and whose health—with proper diet, exercise, and overall care—should remain good throughout what can be a long and happy life. This chapter covers the basics of what you should know to provide good overall care, including how to find the best veterinarian for you and your Beagle; what you need to know about the annual exam; what vaccinations your Beagle needs (and when); what breed-specific illnesses you need to be aware of; how to handle general illnesses; and what kinds of alternative therapies might help your Beagle.

Finding a Veterinarian

It may not seem like it, but your choice of veterinarian is important. Along with you and your family, your veterinarian is responsible for giving your Beagle the best care possible. The only way to do that is for her to get to know your Beagle and to get to know you. You speak for your Beagle, and you are the first one to assess his condition. The advice your veterinarian provides for you will start with what you tell her, and after a thorough examination, proceed from there.

Like a family doctor or your child's pediatrician, your veterinarian should be someone you feel comfortable calling any time you have any kind of concern about your Beagle. She should be responsive and attentive to your calls. When you visit your veterinarian, you should feel that you are getting her full attention and that your Beagle is being truly cared for, not simply processed. The veterinarian's facilities and staff should be equally conscientious and responsive. You will be able to tell if the veterinary technicians truly care for animals by the way they handle them. If your Beagle ever needs to stay overnight at the vet's, can you feel confident that he will be well taken care of in a safe and sanitary environment?

So, how do you find such a person and place? If you got a puppy from a reputable breeder who lives near you, ask her for a recommendation. Breeders work closely with vets, and having their recommendation is certainly a good starting point, although it doesn't mean that you'll be comfortable with their choice.

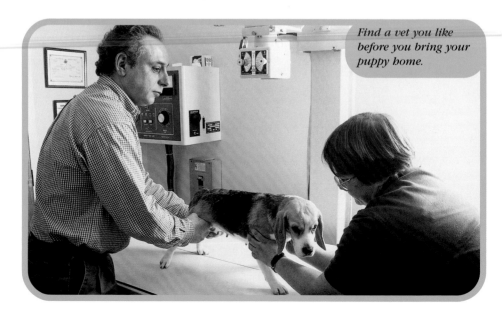

Find a vet you like before you bring your puppy home.

Depending on how many veterinarians have practices in your area, you can call and make appointments to stop by and speak with them before you even get your Beagle. The ones who truly care should be happy to answer your questions and should be pleased that you are making an effort to make the right decision. An office that can't find the time to meet with you if you don't have an animal probably isn't going to be as attentive as you need.

Another option is to ask a friend or acquaintance in your area for a recommendation. Ask someone who you know takes really good care of their dog(s); chances are they have found someone they really like and trust. The American Animal Hospital Association (AAHA) has a list of affiliated veterinarians by city and state on its website, www.aahanet.org.

Visiting the Office

When you visit the veterinarian for the first time, pay close attention to the surroundings and the people visiting the office. Do people seem fairly relaxed? Is the staff attentive? If you see a doctor speaking with someone, does she seem genuine? Ask the people waiting what they think of the clinic. Be wary of a clinic that has too many veterinarians on staff. Their policy may be that your Beagle will be seen by an available veterinarian when you make an appointment, not necessarily the

SENIOR DOG TIP

Your Senior Beagle's Health

With the help of improved diets, advanced veterinary care, and the status of true family member and friend, dogs are experiencing longer and fuller lives. Good health in the senior years—which hopefully may last nearly a decade—begins with doing everything to ensure good health from puppyhood. It all comes down to the care and attention you pay your Beagle from the day you bring him into your life. Proper diet, exercise, grooming, and lifestyle are elemental aspects of longevity. That said, things change as your Beagle ages. From joint pain to impaired vision to forgetfulness to dietary changes, being old has its complications. With your attention and the care of a trusted veterinarian, do your best for your Beagle and both of you will reap the rewards for as long as you're together.

person you saw last time. Or if you want to see the same vet, it may be more difficult to get an appointment. This isn't good for you or your Beagle in the long run.

Your vet will give your Beagle a thorough going over at his yearly exam.

When you find someone you like, you'll know it. Of course, that person will need to prove herself over time with you and your Beagle, but at least you should get off to the best start possible.

The Annual Examination

If you've taken the time to find a veterinarian you're enthusiastic about, you'll be eager to bring in your puppy for his first visit. That's the way it should be! If you're okay with it, your puppy will sense it, and even though all dogs fret when they go to the veterinarian's office because it's filled with the smells and sounds of anxious and strange animals, they can at least turn to you as a source of calm.

Your puppy's first well visit will get him started on the road to annual examinations. These visits are critical for the long-term health of your Beagle because even if your dog seems perfectly fine, an examination by a trained professional can turn up problems you wouldn't know your Beagle had without it.

Eyes, Ears, and Nose

A veterinarian will routinely check your dog's eyes, ears, and nose. The vet is looking for any unusual discharges or discolorations. She will use special instruments that shine light into areas you wouldn't normally be able to examine. Contagious illnesses often manifest themselves first through eye and ear discharge. Dull, lifeless eyes can be a sign of internal parasites or a more serious condition. With an otoscope, the vet can look deep into your Beagle's ears for telltale signs of mites or any discharge or inflammation that could mean your dog has an infection of some sort.

Mouth

Your veterinarian will examine your Beagle's teeth and gums. Puppy teeth should be sparkly white, and your Beagle's bite should be level. If it's not, it doesn't mean that your dog won't be a great friend, but it may mean that you have to pay special attention to how his jaw develops as he grows so that he can eat, drink, and breathe properly. Your Beagle's gums always should be pink and healthy looking. Swelling, discoloration, soreness, or bad breath are all conditions that need to be addressed and remedied.

Heart and Lungs

Veterinarians are aware of what a healthy heart and lungs sound like. Chest congestion can mean that your Beagle has anything from kennel cough to heartworm. Abnormal breathing patterns need to be assessed and monitored. The same goes for any kind of heartbeat abnormality. Your veterinarian will take note of these things so that there is a record for future reference.

Skin and Coat

You may think that your Beagle's skin and coat are just fine, even if he's shedding a lot or itching. Something you may think is just part of being a dog may mean that your Beagle's skin is under attack. A careful veterinary examination can reveal ticks, fleas or other external parasites you may not have noticed. Any hot spots, raw areas from itching, or other oddities should be addressed.

Abdomen, Back, and Tail

By running her hands over the rest of your

Neutering Your Beagle

One of the best things you can do for the health of your Beagle and for the well-being of the canine population is to neuter your dog. Of course, we all think that our dog is the very best there is and that having his or her puppies will keep him or her with us longer or bring the same joy to others, but truthfully, there is happiness to be had with any pup. Don't contribute to the pet overpopulation problem because you're blinded by love.

On the health side, your spayed female will be less prone to diseases of her reproductive system, and best of all, you'll never have to worry about stray males prowling your yard, howling outside your window, or racing down the street after your girl. You won't have to worry about the stain and odor of heat cycles, and you won't have to worry about the many things that can go wrong with a pregnancy and the whelping of puppies. If you have a male, neutering him will lower his tendency to be territorial, both by marking everywhere and posturing with other males. You won't have to worry about diseases of the reproductive system, and you won't have to worry about bringing a female into the house.

Beagle's body, your veterinarian is feeling for anything unusual in the area of his stomach and other internal organs, as well as the spine and skeleton. Signs of pain or even mild discomfort can alert your vet to a larger problem. The vet will examine the area around your Beagle's anus and genitals for any swelling or discoloration.

Finally, the Feet

Last but not least, the vet will examine your Beagle's paws. He should have firm pads and smooth skin between his toes. If you're having trouble trimming your Beagle's nails, ask your vet to do it for you and to show you how.

Time to Learn

With a complete check from head to toe, your veterinarian can advise you on things to think about and look for based on what she is seeing and feeling. If your Beagle's skin and coat are dry or flaky, your vet may suggest that you supplement his food with a fatty rich oil like flax or fish oil. If his ears are inflamed, the vet may suggest a special cleanser to see if that helps. Your exam time is also a good time to review any other concerns you may have with your vet. You should leave feeling like you've learned more about your Beagle.

All About Vaccinations

One reason veterinarians put dogs on a schedule of annual visits is so that they can update their "shots," or vaccines. For many years, a combination vaccine meant to protect your dog against a host of infectious diseases was given annually. Times have changed.

The veterinary community is actively reexamining its approach to annual booster shots. The primary concern of veterinarians is that the animals in their care are safeguarded against potentially fatal diseases. Animal owners are equally concerned that their beloved friends are protected. But are combination shots the best way to go? And do they need to be given every year like clockwork? Your veterinarian will have a strong opinion on this, and it's important to discuss this issue with her.

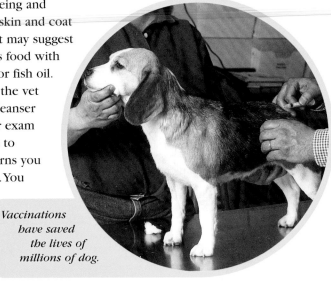

Vaccinations have saved the lives of millions of dog.

As someone who must be the first line of care and defense for your dog, just like with yourself or your family, you should learn as much as you can about the pros and cons of the vaccine controversy so that you can listen to your veterinarian as someone who's educated on the issue. Even doctors are wrong sometimes, or they can be overcautious.

Diseases to Protect Against

What everyone agrees on is that it's essential to give a puppy all of his shots, and the combination vaccine available today is recommended. Called the DHLPP shot, it protects against distemper, hepatitis, leptospirosis, parvovirus, and parainfluenza.

- **Distemper** is the number-one killer of unvaccinated dogs. It is a virus that attacks the nervous system, and left untreated, distemper can cause permanent damage to the brain or central nervous system.

- **Hepatitis** is a virus that attacks the liver and kidneys, causing acute diarrhea that eventually leads to death. Hepatitis is highly contagious and cannot be cured.

- **Leptospirosis** also damages the liver and kidneys, but it's caused by a spirochete transmitted in the urine of infected dogs or vermin (like rats). Although leptospirosis can be treated, infected dogs will suffer greatly until the spirochete is killed off, and even if they live, they can

FAMILY-FRIENDLY TIP

A Family Visit to the Vet

Taking your whole family to the veterinarian for routine visits is a great way to participate together in the care of your four-footed family member. Kids typically enjoy meeting the other pets who are waiting to see the vet, and when it's your turn to meet with the doggy doctor, if you have the whole family there, she usually will take extra time to explain what's happening.

What may start off as a good idea can go terribly wrong if you aren't considerate and polite at the veterinarian's office. Remind your kids that not all the animals want to be petted and that some of them may be quite sick. When you're in a private room waiting for the vet, don't let your children touch or play with anything. Let them know that unless the doctor says it's okay, her "office" and the things in it are private.

Keep in mind that your Beagle probably won't like being at the vet's. It smells funny and makes him nervous. The calmer the whole family is, the better he'll feel.

remain a carrier of the disease, able to pass it along to other dogs.

- **Parvovirus** surfaced as a "new" disease in the early 1980s, and because the vaccine didn't yet exist, many puppies were lost to it. A virus that infects puppies and young dogs, it is extremely virulent and can leave an otherwise healthy pup dead in a day.

- **Parainfluenza** is a highly contagious disease that's part virus and part bacteria. It attacks the lungs, resulting in a hacking cough.

When you know what these diseases can do, you know why veterinarians would be negligent not to protect animals against them.

There are other diseases that veterinarians vaccinate against. These include:

- **Coronavirus,** which is a virus similar to parvovirus.

- **Bordetella,** also known as "kennel cough" because it is spread where many strange dogs come together, like kennels or dog shows.

- **Lyme disease**, which is caused by bacteria spread through infected tick bites.

- **Rabies,** a potentially fatal and highly contagious virus that's transmitted through the saliva of an infected animal and can be transmitted to humans. Rabies is the only vaccine that your dog must be given by law to protect your dog, your family, and the community.

Vaccinating Past Puppyhood

Advances are made in medical and veterinary technology all the time, and we are fortunate to live in a time where blood tests can be done to assess the amount of a vaccine (or other substance) still in the dog's blood. These tests, called titers, are routine and fairly accurate. They can alert your veterinarian to whether your Beagle still has enough protection from, say, parainfluenza, to put off giving him a shot for it until a later date. If your dog isn't kenneled often or doesn't mix with large groups of strange dogs often, he may not need a shot for bordetella. However, if you need to kennel him for a few weeks while you vacation, the kennel should require that he be vaccinated for it, for the protection of your Beagle and the other boarders.

Rather than routinely vaccinating your older or aging Beagle against everything, discuss with your vet which vaccinations are essential.

Thankfully, Beagles are generally a healthy breed.

Beagle-Specific Illnesses

As a breed, the Beagle has been spared some of the inherent diseases that affect other breeds. Thank goodness! Another piece of good news: An exceptional resource for Beagle owners is the National Beagle Club's website, where there is an extensive section on health problems. Visit it at http://clubs.akc.org. Find out as much as you can about the medical background of your Beagle so that you can be on the lookout for tell-tale signs of anything that has been a problem for any of your Beagle's relatives. The most common— cherry eye, epilepsy, glaucoma, heart murmurs, and disc problems—are discussed here.

Cherry Eye

Cherry eye is a swelling of the Beagle's third eyelid, causing it to protrude. It's the result of an infection and is treated with antibiotics, and if necessary, surgery.

Epilepsy

Epilepsy is a disease of the brain and central nervous system that causes seizures. These can be either mild (petit mal) and almost undetectable (the Beagle appears to be slightly disoriented for a lingering moment) or severe (grand mal). A Beagle experiencing a severe seizure will lose muscle control, stiffen, and convulse. Even though it may only last a few minutes, it is extremely frightening to observe. Epilepsy must be controlled with medication.

Glaucoma

Glaucoma results when there is too much pressure behind the eye, causing damage to the optic nerve that results in decreased vision and eventual blindness if not treated. Treatment is with eye drops, or if there is a chance of restoring sight to the eye, surgery. Knowing about any history of this in your Beagle's bloodlines and making sure that your veterinarian checks your Beagle's eyes regularly are your best lines of defense.

Heart Murmurs

Heart murmurs are irregular patterns of the heartbeat that can be caused by a variety of conditions. Identified diseases include dilated cardiomyopathy (DCM) and pulmonic stenosis (PS). Early detection of a heart murmur will help your veterinarian decide the best course of treatment. You may not even know that your dog has this problem until your veterinarian detects it during an annual physical, which is why it's so important to keep those appointments. Treatment of a heart murmur will depend on what your veterinarian thinks is best for your Beagle.

Intervertebral Disk Disease

Intervertebral disk disease affects Beagles typically when they're three years old and older, which is when the disks ("cushions" between the vertebrae and under the spinal cord) begin to dehydrate, losing their flexibility and putting pressure on the spinal cord. Yelping when you pick up your Beagle or reluctance to jump or go up or down the stairs may be signs. If your Beagle is diagnosed with invertebral disk disease, your veterinarian will recommend medical therapy or surgery. The former uses pain relievers and anti-inflammatories to relieve the pressure and pain. The objective of surgery is to permanently relieve the condition.

General Health Concerns

In between routine veterinary visits, there are some things that affect all dogs that you need to be on the lookout for so that your Beagle stays healthy. Because a Beagle is a dog who thrives in the great outdoors (in fact, getting him outside and allowing him a safe opportunity to follow his nose is one of the best things you can do for his mental health), you will need to beware of parasites, both internal and external.

Beagles

Good breeding plays an essential role in health.

Internal Parasites

Otherwise known as "worms," internal parasites enter your Beagle's system through his skin or something he eats or drinks. Once inside, the parasite finds the warm environment it's looking for to complete its life cycle and grow. Just the thought of worms growing inside your Beagle should give you the creeps; the reality of the situation is even uglier. Fortunately, much is known about internal parasites, and routine preventive care is simple and cost effective, and it works. Learn what to look for and do, and you should never have to worry about worms.

Heartworm

This is a parasite that grows in the vessels of the heart, and if untreated, eventually blocks the heart and leads to heart failure and death. The parasite is transmitted through infected mosquitoes when they bite a dog. It can take several months for the worms to find their way to the heart and start growing. Signs of heartworm include a chronic cough, weight loss, and fatigue. Your veterinarian will recommend that you put your Beagle on a routine heartworm preventive to protect him from ever being infected. He will need to have a blood test to be sure that he isn't already infected. The medicine is a tasty pill typically given once a month. If it's too late and your Beagle gets heartworm, he can be treated, although the treatment is painful and not always completely effective.

After puppies are born, a routine puppy wormer is necessary.

61

Hookworm

These are small worms that attach themselves to your dog's intestinal lining where they suck blood. Dogs infected with hookworm become anemic and will have pale gums. Their stool also may be bloody or resemble tar. Puppies are sometimes born with hookworms (and roundworms), and as long as the breeder gave them a routine puppy dewormer, the problem should have been resolved. Hookworms get into your dog through his feet if he's spending any time in an unsanitary environment. Treatment (the appropriate medicine) for infected dogs is effective.

Roundworm

In reality, roundworms are long and thin, not round at all. They can grow up

vomiting. Immediate treatment is necessary to kill off all worms.

Taking Your Beagle's Temperature

If your Beagle seems lethargic or out of sorts—and certainly if he misses a meal—you should take his temperature. A dog's normal rectal temperature is 100.5° to 102.5°F (38° to 39°C). To take his temperature, ask someone to help you. You'll need someone to hold his head so that you can work with his rear end—he may not be too happy about the process!

Shake down a rectal thermometer or restart it so that there is no reading. Apply some petroleum jelly to the part that needs to go inside your dog so that it goes in easier. You may want to tie a string around the thermometer before you start so that if your Beagle squirms or sits and the thermometer goes all the way in, you'll be able to remove it easily. Once the thermometer is in, wait for either the beeping that indicates the temperature level is reached, or give a mercury-based thermometer about two minutes. Remove the thermometer and take note of the temperature. Report anything abnormal to your veterinarian immediately.

Tapeworm

The tapeworm is a segmented parasite that feeds in the host's intestine. It is typically transmitted through fleas and dead animals. For an active hunting Beagle who may well come upon a rabbit, rodent, or deer carcass and think he's the luckiest hound in the world, a tapeworm infestation can be a likely scenario. Fortunately, they are the least harmful to your dog, although they must still be eradicated by giving the proper medication. Signs of tapeworm include the appearance of small rice-like segments around your Beagle's anus or in his stool. Of course, keeping his environment flea-free is a must.

Whipworm

Though not commonly discussed, whipworms are the most prevalent

to 6 inches (15 cm) long and are the width of pencil lead. They multiply quickly, and if left untreated, can cause sudden death, particularly in a puppy. They are actually present in all newborn pups, whether their mother was dewormed or not, which is why a routine puppy dewormer is necessary. Roundworms can easily infect humans as well. An infected puppy or dog will have a dull coat, pot-bellied appearance, and overly sweet breath with possible diarrhea, coughing, and parasite in dogs in North America. Part of the reason is that they are hardy and can survive for up to five years in the environment; another is that they are transmitted through the feces of other infected animals, so any Beagle who eats poop can become infected. Whipworms feed in the lower intestine, where they can live and feed for months undetected. Infected dogs become anemic but may otherwise appear normal. A diagnosis can be made by examining a stool sample, and treatment involves medication. Whipworms are another reason why it's so important that dog owners pick up after their dogs and keep their yards clean.

External Parasites

These are the nasty things that attack your Beagle from the outside: fleas, mites, ringworm, and ticks. They are all dangerous and need to be guarded against vigilantly. The sooner you notice and get rid of them, the better off your dog, your family, and your house and yard will be.

Fleas

These nasty bugs have a life cycle that can keep them present in your home and on your dog even when you think you've gotten rid of them. Because they reproduce so rapidly, by the time you see a flea on your dog, it means that there are already eggs laid in your house— wherever your dog rests—so you will need to treat your entire environment. Another perplexing thing about fleas is that they can develop resistance to treatment methods.

Keeping your dog flea-free is big business, and depending on where you live, you may need to tend to the problem all year or seasonally. Your veterinarian can discuss which preventive treatment methods she thinks are best for your Beagle, from those that work from the inside out to

63

Check your Beagle for fleas after he's been outside

those that kill or repel fleas from the outside. Keep in mind that treatment can have side effects. Learn about whatever chemicals you're putting on your Beagle, and decide whether they're worth it overall. Remember that fleas and other bugs tend to gravitate toward animals with more compromised immune systems, so keeping your Beagle healthy from the inside out with the proper diet, and possibly supplements, could be all you need in your battle against fleas—oh, and a flea comb.

Going through your Beagle's fur after outdoor jaunts with a fine-tined flea comb will ensure that any pesky critter that landed on your dog will not find a home on him. Pay particular attention to the areas around your Beagle's head, neck, groin, and tail.

Crush any fleas the comb isolates with your fingernail, or dip the comb in a jar of rubbing alcohol to kill the flea. During flea season, be sure to change your vacuum cleaner bags frequently, and pay close attention to your dog's sleeping areas.

Mites

It's bad enough that these tiny creatures exist at all, but there are actually two forms of them: ear mites and mange mites. All mites burrow into the skin and irritate tissue. Ear mites infect the ears, and if your Beagle is scratching at or shaking his head frequently, he should be checked for these. Mange mites infect the skin, and present as either demodectic mange or sarcoptic mange. The former causes hair loss, itching, and an overall "moth-eaten" appearance. It tends to manifest when the dog's immune system is compromised and is therefore best prevented with sound nutrition and the kind of care discussed in this book. Sarcoptic mange causes intense itching that results in red, raw patches or bumps that become

After hunting around in the brush, you may find a tick on your Beagle.

First Aid

A medical emergency is the last thing you want to think about, but when it happens and you have to deal with it, you'll get through it better if you're prepared. If you don't have one in the house already, now is the time to put a first-aid kit together—for you and your dog. First, designate a container where you will put all the things that should be in the kit, and place it in a special place. Even if it's not an emergency, knowing where the antibiotic ointment is should your Beagle cut himself will help you treat him sooner and more calmly. Here's what should be in your canine first-aid kit:

- Antibiotic ointment
- Adhesive tape (1–2 inches [2–5 cm] wide)
- Buffered, enteric, or children's aspirin (not ibuprofen or acetaminophen)
- Gauze pads and rolls
- Cotton balls
- Hydrogen peroxide 3% solution
- Rubbing alcohol
- Rectal thermometer
- Small, sharp scissors
- Tweezers
- Disposable latex gloves (several pairs)
- Pair of old stockings (for making a temporary muzzle)
- The phone numbers of your veterinarian, a poison control center, and the emergency hospital (along with directions)

crusty as the dog continues to itch. Fortunately, sarcoptic mange responds well to treatment.

Ringworm

While not technically a worm (it's a fungus), ringworm is an external parasite—and one that's highly contagious. Infected dogs and people spread the disease when ringworm spores drop from their hair or skin. Feeding on dead surface skin and hair cells, ringworm creates an itchy, scaly,

bald patch. It can be treated with specialized topical ointment, but it's tough to eliminate because it survives so well. During treatment, fastidious attention to the hygiene of the dog's environment is critical.

Ticks

There are three kinds of ticks: the wood tick, the brown dog tick, and the deer tick. The brown dog tick is the most common and looks like what it sounds like. It's the one that's typically the size of a small bead, and is flat and brown. It can carry Rocky Mountain spotted fever, tularemia, encephalitis, and possibly Lyme disease. The wood tick is the largest tick, and is gray and about the width of a pencil. The deer tick is tiny—the size of a fleck of pepper when not engorged—and is the primary host for Lyme disease. Ticks are bad for pets and people.

There are tick preventives similar to those for fleas, and their effectiveness and use should be discussed with your veterinarian. You are bound to find ticks on your Beagle (or yourself) at some time, so you need to know what to do about them. First, remove them with tweezers if possible, being sure to grab by the head, close to the skin. You want to remove as much of the tick as possible as cleanly as possible. Once removed, put the tick into a jar of rubbing alcohol to kill it. When it is dead, flush it down the toilet. Clean the bite spot with hydrogen peroxide followed by a dab of antibiotic ointment. Keep an eye on the spot. If you notice redness or swelling around it, make an appointment to have your veterinarian look at it. The sooner treatment begins for a possible infection, the better.

Other Problems

Accidents

Beagles have accidents just like the rest of us—and can be treated for most of them just like the rest of us. Cuts and scrapes (when not severe) can be treated with antibiotic ointment and bandaging; burns should tended by a veterinarian because they can be extremely sensitive; apply a soothing baking-soda paste to stings; general pain can be alleviated with buffered aspirin or children's aspirin (no ibuprofen or acetaminophen); and localized pain

Keep calm in an emergency—your Beagle is counting on you.

should be monitored for severity. Whenever you aren't sure what to do, call your veterinarian!

Allergies

As a breed, Beagles are fairly allergy-free, though of course there are individual cases. Allergies can be brought on by a host of things, from the saliva in a flea bite to something in his food to a chemical in your carpet. Once properly identified, the allergen should be removed from your dog's environment.

Diarrhea

Like you, your hound may occasionally experience diarrhea. You can give him an anti-diarrhea medication like Pepto-Bismol or Kaopectate to bring it under control, and you'll want to feed him a bland diet of boiled or baked chicken and rice along with plenty of water. If he doesn't bounce back fairly quickly, take him to the vet.

Ear Infections

With their long, droopy ears, Beagles are more prone to infection, and regular ear cleaning must be a part of the regular care you give your dog. (See Chapter 4.) While you're cleaning, or even in between cleanings, if you notice a foul smell, unusual discharge, or swelling or redness, make an appointment to have the ear examined by your veterinarian.

Top Ten Sources of Poisonings in Pets

The American Society for the Prevention of Cruelty to Animals (ASPCA) operates an Animal Poison Control Center that boosts a 24/7 hotline to assist pet owners with questions about poisoning (1-888-426-4435). In 2005, the center received more than 100,000 calls. These were pet owners' top 10 sources of poisonings, by frequency.

1. Human medications, including painkillers, cold medicines, prescriptions, and dietary supplements
2. Insecticides like those used to kill fleas and ticks
3. Rodenticides (poison for mice and rats)
4. Veterinary medications, which need to be given strictly according to the directions and under a veterinarian's supervision
5. Household cleaners
6. Herbicides
7. Plants
8. Chocolate
9. Home improvement products
10. Fertilizers

The ASPCA is an excellent resource for all kinds of questions and concerns about potential toxins. Visit their website at www.aspca.org to learn more.

You might want to explore alternative therapies for your Beagle.

Poisoning

If you suspect that your Beagle ingested something poisonous, call your veterinarian immediately. If it is after hours, call a poison control hotline. The ASPCA has been operating the Animal Poison Control Center for several decades and receives hundreds of thousands of calls about potential poisonings. To reach the ASPCA Animal Poison Control Center, call 1-888-426-4435. For more information on the ASPCA Animal Poison Control Center, visit www.aspca.org/apcc.

It is critical that you identify the source of the poison because the proper treatment depends on it. If your veterinarian recommends it, you can induce vomiting by giving your dog a hydrogen peroxide 3% solution. Use 1 teaspoon per 10 pounds (4.5 kg) of body weight, and take your dog outside. He should throw up within 15 to 20 minutes. Bring a plastic bag because there may be traces of the

Hot Spots

Also called moist eczema or summer sores, hot spots are caused by a variety of bacteria, which can enter the skin when it's exposed in any number of ways, from swimming to rolling in wet grass. Hot spots tend to appear almost overnight, and cause instant hair loss and itching. While treatment is available, usually in the form of an anti-inflammatory, the itching can become almost a self-perpetuating habit for your Beagle. Work with your veterinarian to find the best solution.

poisonous substance in the vomit. Your veterinarian may need this. Because inducing vomiting is potentially dangerous, only do it upon your veterinarian's advice.

Vomiting

Dogs vomit for a number of reasons, so seeing your dog throw up may not mean that there is anything seriously wrong. Dogs like to eat grass (although no one knows exactly why), which they typically vomit later. While unpleasant, this isn't cause for concern. If your Beagle plays hard after a big meal, he may throw up part of it—and may try to eat it again. If infrequent, this is no cause for concern either. If the vomiting follows a period of coughing or hacking, and seems to happen often, it could be a sign of a parasitic infection. This, or vomiting accompanied by weight loss or a high fever, warrants a trip to the vet.

Alternative Therapies

For all of us, the approach to disease is being addressed more and more holistically. That means that rather than simply introducing something that will kill or mask the symptoms of the illness, the actual root of the illness is being explored and treated as well. For example, although there are numerous ways to kill or treat parasites, there are also ways to prevent them from being a problem for your dog (and you) by boosting the immune system, keeping the environment clean, and striving for overall robust health. You can't be laissez-faire about treating a condition that could leave your Beagle critically ill while you introduce kelp to his diet, for example, but you can explore all the ways that a problem can be manifesting or can be supported during treatment by alternative therapies. Canine health care has extended to acupuncture, chiropractic, reiki, herbal therapy, homeopathy, aromatherapy, and more.

Good health practices will keep your Beagle a member of the family for many years.

Chapter 6

Being Good

The introduction to a chapter on training a Beagle must begin with a bit of a lecture on expectations—what you can, can't, should, and shouldn't expect from your hound. What you can and should expect is that your Beagle has the brains and ability to figure out what you want him to do. What you can't and shouldn't expect is that he's going to give you the eager attitude and determination of a retriever, for example. A Beagle is hardwired to be an independent thinker, and as you've learned from previous chapters, he's driven by his nose. These elements of his nature affect his attention level and response to training.

You can—and should—expect that the positive training methods explained in this book will get you the results you need. You can't—and shouldn't—expect that your Beagle will master the training too quickly. Every dog is an individual and learns at a different rate. You may move to the head of the class with your Beagle and have him doing tricks in a matter of weeks. If so, that's wonderful for you and your dog! Then again, you may become frustrated when something that seems simple doesn't go so well. If that's the case, forgive your Beagle his inclination to be amused by other things, try to determine where the breakdown is happening, and keep trying. You definitely can expect that your efforts will be rewarded!

Socialize your Beagle to calm, gentle children.

Why Socialization Is Critical

For the emotional health of your Beagle—as well as the physical safety of him and your family—it is critical to get him out into the world where he can meet and experience as many kinds of people, other animals, and environments as possible. Every positive interaction will boost his self-confidence and make him less afraid. Socialization exposes him to safe and unsafe situations with you there to assure or to rescue him so that he can better handle all other experiences.

To socialize your puppy or dog, take him out and ask kind strangers (and of course, friends, neighbors, co-workers, and others you trust) to say his name and give him a tasty treat. This teaches him that strange-looking giants looming over him are usually friendly, and in fact often give him yummy stuff. Great places to do this are puppy kindergarten classes (now offered by most trainers in conjunction with their regular classes for older dogs), mall parking lots, national parks, children's sporting events or practices, and the local downtown shopping area. These outings also will give you clues about what may trigger your dog to react defensively or abnormally. Take note and work to desensitize your dog to these hot spots.

Housetraining

Successful housetraining begins with a schedule and boundaries. The schedule is important because it lets you (and your Beagle, eventually) know what to expect. You can anticipate that your Beagle will need to eliminate shortly after he eats; almost immediately after a nap or sleeping through the night; at times of excitement, like playtime; and every so often in between. All you need to do is meet these needs, reinforce his going potty where you want him to go, and be consistent. It sounds easy, but the truth is that people get distracted and forget about taking their dog out, and next thing they know, the dog has an accident. (Chapter 7 discusses how to handle a house soiling problem.)

Boundaries help to prevent accidents by confining your Beagle to an area he shouldn't want to soil because he also sleeps there, and to a place that's easy for you to clean. The ideal boundaries are established by a crate, although a dog-proofed room like a kitchen or mud room secured with a baby gate also can do the job.

Why a Crate Is Great

A crate almost guarantees quicker success with housetraining. How? A properly outfitted crate will serve as your dog's own "den,"

a place where he will sleep, play, and possibly eat—not a place he'll want to soil. Place the crate in an area where your family spends a lot of time, like the kitchen or family room.

What a crate is not is a dog prison. Never put your Beagle in the crate in anger and "lock the door" to leave him there. If you use the crate as a place for punishing your dog, he will not see it as a safe den; instead, he will view it as a frightening place, and he will protest being confined there by howling and trying to chew it apart, which could cause serious injury.

Getting Used to the Crate

First, your Beagle will need to be made to feel comfortable and safe in the crate. Put a soft towel or blanket inside—something easy to wash in case

73

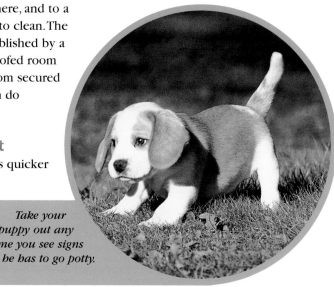

Take your puppy out any time you see signs he has to go potty.

of an accident. At first, leave the door open, bring your Beagle to the crate, and toss some tasty treats inside. Praise him for exploring. Do this a few times, encouraging him to go in and out and investigate without feeling trapped. After a few easy ins and outs, as he goes in after a treat, quietly close the door behind him, praise him for being

in the crate, and pause a minute before opening the door to let him out. If he starts to cry, don't respond in any way and avoid eye contact. He'll eventually pause, and this is when you should pop the door and let him out. You want him to learn that being quiet is his cue to freedom, not crying.

Once your dog knows that his crate is a good place, begin to use it to reinforce your housetraining. Start feeding your dog in his crate with the door closed. When he's finished, open the door, put on his leash, pick up his bowl, and take him outside to eliminate.

Responding to Accidents

It's natural to become upset when you discover an accident in the house, and many of us grew up thinking that the dog should be dragged over to the site of the accident, forced to confront it, and spanked and scolded for it.

Wrong. Unless you catch your dog in the act and can respond with a sharp "No!" while immediately bringing him to his proper potty place, your dog will not understand what he did wrong. Instead, he'll learn that you can be very scary and unpredictable, which may in fact increase the incidence of accidents. So what should you do? You're allowed to be upset, but take it out on the accident itself. Curse while you clean it up, then ask yourself why it might have happened. Did you skip an

Training Treats

Finding a treat that your Beagle will respond to enthusiastically shouldn't be much of a problem. Beagles are motivated by food, and you'll find that the really yummy stuff like cheese, cooked meat, dried liver, and special doggy treats will all get his undivided attention. The purpose of the treats is to keep him focused on you and to learn that the reward comes when he does something you like. To work effectively, the treats you prepare for training sessions have to be small. Your dog should eat them in one easy bite and look for more. Remember that treats are food, and the calories count. You may need to cut back on the amounts you give your Beagle for breakfast and dinner to compensate for the additional calories.

exercise time? Is your Beagle excited or upset about something? Did you forget to confine your puppy while you were busy with something else?

Obviously, accidents that involve diarrhea or bloody discharges are cause for concern, and you should notify your veterinarian. For best results, don't use household cleaners on a dog accident. Use an enzymatic pet stain and odor cleaner, and follow the instructions.

Don't Let Him Train You

Ideally, you should train your Beagle to pee and poop around the same spot, and you want him to do both fairly soon when you get outside. If he does, he gets extra time outside. If he doesn't, back inside until it's time—which may be immediately. What you don't want to do is establish a routine where you go out and you need to take him for a ten-minute walk before he'll even think about doing his business. He may begin to do this if you bring him back inside too quickly. Beagles live for being outside and sniffing around, and if you simply whisk him in and out when it's potty time, he'll figure out that he needs to stall you somehow.

Basic Training

When it comes to the foundation for canine manners, there are essentially five things all dogs need to master: *sit, stay, down, come,* and *heel* (walk nicely on a

Consistency is the key to housetraining your puppy.

leash). Armed with a buckle collar, leash, and baggy of the yummiest treats, you're almost ready to begin. To motivate your Beagle, you must make yourself irresistible. If you approach training with a shred of doubt or worry, your sensitive Beagle will pick up on it, and you'll be giving him the excuse he needs to do something else.

When you begin training, make it as easy for your Beagle as possible by working in a small area with few distractions. (The kitchen is a good place to train because you spend a lot of time there anyway, so it's good for your dog to know that certain things are expected of him there.) Train in the early morning before the house gets too busy, for example. If the kids want to watch, that's fine, but let them know that they need to be quiet so that your

Finding a Trainer

The information in this chapter will help you understand the training process and instruct you in teaching basic manners. Even with this, you may want to take your Beagle to a training class where he will be further socialized and where you'll both learn from the instructor and from the others in the class. Don't trust just any trainer, though. The wrong trainer can do much more harm than good. The best source for a reliable trainer is the Association of Pet Dog Trainers (APDT), a national group that certifies its trainers and encourages the use of positive training methods. Research the organization and find members who are trainers in your area by contacting the APDT at 1-800-PET-DOGS or www.apdt.com.

it's practical. Once your Beagle knows the *sit*, you can ask him to do it anytime or anywhere you need him to sit quietly at your side. Begin with your Beagle in his collar and on leash, and keep him in a fairly confined space that's relatively distraction-free. You don't need to hold your dog by the leash to do this, but if he can't focus, it's handy to have it on him just in case. With a *really* tasty treat in your hand, like a small chunk of cheese, cooked meat, hot dog, or piece of popcorn, tease him with it so that his full attention is on you. When he is fully focused on you and the treat, dog can focus on what you're trying to teach him.

Training sessions need only last a few minutes. You don't want to frustrate yourself or your dog. If it's going well, end on a good note; if it's going badly, stop and reevaluate what you're doing. Do several short training sessions throughout the day instead of working with your Beagle for a solid half hour every day.

Teaching *Sit*

This is the first thing you'll want to teach your Beagle because it's easy, and

Food rewards are an excellent way to train your Beagle.

bring the treat to his nose. Then, as he's working to get at it with his mouth, slowly lift it up between his eyes and above his head. Don't say anything as you're luring him through this. As his face moves up to follow the treat, his bottom will drop and he'll naturally sit. As soon as his bottom goes into a sit, give him the treat and say "Good sit!" Do this two or three times in a row (not more than that), and do it several times a day.

The *sit* can be easy to work into your daily routine. For example, ask your dog to sit before you open the door to come back inside your house after a potty break and walk. Ask him to sit before feeding him his meals. Ask him to sit when you come home—and don't pet him until he does! Each time he sits in these situations, let him know what a wonderful and smart Beagle he is by rewarding him with a treat or a genuine show of affection. Say "Okay" to let him know that he finished what you asked him.

Teaching *Stay*

Stay is a fundamental request because you need it so often. Is your eager Beagle anxious to go outside for his morning and evening walks? *Stay* (and *wait*) will keep him from bolting out the door. How about when you go somewhere in the car—does your dog whine and excitedly try to escape from the vehicle as you're wrestling to get his leash on? Asking him to stay (and wait) will make the process less hectic.

FAMILY-FRIENDLY TIP

When Your Children Want to Train Your Beagle

Most children are eager to help to train the family dog, especially when they see how easy it looks for you. They can be equally successful with it, depending on their age and temperament. Children younger than four should be held in your lap while you work with your Beagle so that you can help to control when and where the treat is released to the dog. A hungry, frustrated Beagle may be too exuberant in taking the treat, and a young child can be frightened by an open mouth coming toward her. In your lap, you can help to guide and direct the process.

Depending on how well you trust the children or your Beagle, you can let grade-schoolers and older children work directly with your dog. Show them what to do, and be sure to supervise in case there are any surprises. Chances are they'll be so thrilled to get responses from your Beagle that they'll want to learn more and more things. Also, if they have you as their guide, you'll know that your Beagle is being trained consistently among family members.

Being Good

With treats, and starting from the *sit* position in his collar with the leash attached, open your hand with the palm facing his face and say "Stay." Say it like you mean it—firmly but gently. Count to two to yourself, then say with great enthusiasm "Good stay!" and give him a treat. When you respond enthusiastically and offer the treat, he will probably get up. That's okay for now, as long as he first held a *stay* for a few seconds.

A great time to practice requesting the *stay* is just before meals. If you've been working on *sit* all along, your Beagle should almost be doing that automatically when mealtime comes around. Now, with him in a *sit*, as you're going to put the bowl down, stop, say "Stay," and hold the bowl for a couple of seconds. Then put the bowl on the floor with a "Good stay!" and "Good boy!" Slowly ask more of him in the premeal *sit-stay* until you can ask your dog to sit and stay while you make his dinner and put it on the floor, always releasing with "Good stay, okay" so that he knows that he can break the request and get his food.

For the first few days, even a week if need be, only ask your dog to stay for a couple of seconds at a time. When you're sure he understands, ask him for longer *stays*. Alternate asking for short *stays* and long *stays* to keep the training meaningful and successful.

Teaching *Down*

This is another request that should be taught only when your Beagle is solid with the *sit*. Going down and staying down on request demonstrate real trust on the part of your dog. Earn it, don't force it, and be prepared to repeat, repeat, repeat. With the tastiest of treats, first ask your Beagle to sit. Praise him when he does, but don't give him the treat just yet. Kneel down in front and slightly to the side of him (ask him to sit again if necessary) so that he has room to

Communicating With Your Beagle

Be careful not to allow yourself or others who work with your Beagle to be overly repetitive when asking for a behavior, even when you're in the early stages of training. A dog who hears "Sit, Sit, Siiiit, Sit! Sit, Sit" before he has even done anything will learn either that it's okay not to respond to one word or that your request is a series of words. Ask once, and expect compliance. To make this work, be intent and focused on the request, and use your "I mean business" voice (not to be confused with the "I'm getting upset" voice, which will not get you the result you're looking for). Remember, too, that dogs are especially sensitive to body language. Your moods, your position, and your eye contact all influence how your dog responds to you.

Training teaches your Beagle to pay attention to you.

disposition can test your patience. The fact is that *come* is an important command. Whether it's wanting him to come in from the yard at night after you let him out to do his business, or asking him to come to you at the dog park, or even calling him to join you in another room of the house, when you want (or need) your dog to come, you want him to respond instantly.

To train this important request, your Beagle should have his collar and leash on, and you should work in a room with no distractions. Be sure to have an

bring his front paws and legs down into the *down* position. Hold the treat at his nose, and while he's sniffing it, slowly move your hand down toward the floor and out toward you. You want him to bring his head down and then start moving his paws out so that his elbows come down to and land on the floor. As soon as they do, give the treat with an encouraging, "Good down."

Always work the down from the *sit* position first. Once your Beagle has reached the *down* position and been rewarded, you can release him with an "Okay" so that he gets the idea that *down* only means all the way on the floor, not to the floor and then back up.

Teaching *Come*

This is where your Beagle's "I'm going it alone" or "Something smells good!"

SENIOR DOG TIP

Techniques for Training an Older Dog

If you rescued or adopted an older Beagle, he may be trained—or he may have learned some bad habits. Whether you want to teach him basic manners or undo some undesirable behaviors, the same training principles apply to working with your dog as they do for working with a puppy. Be clear about what you want to teach, work from the beginning, and reward only the behavior you want.

Ignore your Beagle when he's not behaving.

adequate supply of bite-sized tasty treats at the ready. At first, just stand and watch your dog. When he becomes interested in something other than you, say "Snoopy, come" in a high, happy voice, and offer the treat. When he gets *all the way to you* (not at arm's length, as if he's merely curious), give him the treat and say "Good come," then "Okay" so that he knows that he can go do something else again. With a couple of treats discreetly in your hand, walk to a different place in the room, and when he's distracted, call him to come to you again. If he comes right away, praise, treat, and release. Do this a few times, then take off the leash and end the training session.

For the first week or so, keep the distance he has to travel to get to you short so that he can't become overly distracted. The lesson is that when you call, he comes, he gets a treat, and then he can go do something else. When he's coming to you this way 99.9 percent of the time, start lengthening the distances from which you call him. Put him on a longer leash (a 6-foot (1.8-m) cotton lead is great), and always call "Snoopy, come" just once. If you don't get a response, turn away from him and start walking, even if you need to gently pull him to move him in your direction. As he's moving toward you, repeat the request and bring him in to you by holding out the treat. No compliance, no treat.

Teaching *Walk Nicely on Leash*

Your Beagle's very strong instinct to sniff anything and everything around him, and to give chase to things that interest him, are tough to train against. Puppies and dogs learn to pull, lunge, or plant themselves while we're walking them because these behaviors get them what they want, which is usually to get to an interesting scent as quickly as possible, to chase a cat or squirrel, or to stay where the sniffing's good. Life will be more pleasant if he knows that you expect him to walk nicely on leash.

The process of going for a walk begins in the home, when it's time to get the leash on or possibly the collar and the leash. When it's "that time," ask your Beagle to sit while you put on his collar and leash, then say "Okay" to release him as you head for the door. At the door, ask him to sit while you open the door. Only open it if he's sitting. This will be hard for both of you at first, but it's a great

Alternate Rewards

As this chapter suggests, working with tasty treats is the surest and easiest way to get your Beagle's attention while you ask him to get into different positions or try to understand what you want. Once he learns these and you've released him with an enthusiastic "Okay," you may find that he is somewhat worked up from his training session. This is a good time to reward him with other things that he likes. Going for an extended walk is a good way to come off of a training session (and you can practice the sit and walking nicely while you do it). If you will be putting your Beagle in his crate for a while, give him a chew toy that's been stuffed with some peanut butter or soft cheese so that he has something to work at. Play tug-of-war or fetch if he likes these games. These are ways to further associate training time with good times.

habit to get into, and it teaches your dog to sit at the door and wait for what he wants.

Once out the door, ask him to sit again as you close and lock the door. You and your dog will only set out together if he does what you ask. At any time during the walk, ask your Beagle to sit. If he does, give him a treat and a hearty "Good sit," and immediately start walking again. If he doesn't, stop walking and

stand still. When his attention is back on you, ask again. If he's interested in going anywhere, eventually he'll learn that you're in charge of the walk. If he pulls, simply stop dead in your tracks until he doubles back and looks to you for an answer. Ask him to sit, and if he does, reward and move on. You are going to feel silly and awkward doing this, but it will pay off in the end.

Patience, Practice, and Praise!

This is the motto of many dog trainers, and they should know. Like anything new that both of you have to learn, training your Beagle to understand and respond to the five essential requests for good behavior can be as frustrating as it can be rewarding. If you are not in the mood to work with your Beagle, don't. Your bad mood could result in unjustly punishing him, setting both of you back. Work slowly, and trust that this stuff will work. Your Beagle is not a Golden Retriever or a Shetland Sheepdog or a German Shepherd Dog—or even the other Beagle in your training class who always gets things right. He is who he is, and it's your obligation to work with him without comparing him to other dogs.

A terrific benefit of the time you put into training is the deepening of the bond you'll feel with your Beagle as you work through the problems—and successes—together. You will come to know each other very well, and that's a wonderful thing.

Chapter 7

In the
Doghouse

Impossible! Your sweet, lovable hound suddenly so naughty you want to banish him from the house? Has your home become a hound haven where your Beagle calls the shots? With his willingness to please and general good nature, and your commitment to making changes, you can work through this and create the kind of household where peace prevails. It means taking a close look at the issues, spending the time and taking the trouble to really try to correct them, setting some rules, and sticking to the plans.

All dog owners let their canine companions get away with things, and mostly it's because, in the end, a behavior isn't really that bothersome and/or it's mutually enjoyable. These things include letting the dog up on the bed or the sofa (or both), giving in to feeding extra goodies during the day, or permitting excessive barking. Just like everyone raises their children differently, everyone has different rules for their dogs. The difference between something the dog shouldn't do but you let him get away with and something the dog shouldn't do, period, really comes down to how in control of the situation you are. If you're letting him do something because you simply can't stop him, that's a problem.

Common Problems

Canine behavior problems tend to revolve around aggression, barking, begging, chasing, chewing, digging, and house soiling. Beagles can be guilty of any or all of these offenses to certain degrees.

Aggression

If your Beagle lets you know that he doesn't like what you or someone else is doing to him by snarling, growling, raising a lip and glaring at you, or even attempting to bite you, he is both an atypical Beagle and one who is insecure and/or unhappy. This does not apply to a Beagle who responds to someone or something physically hurting him by lashing out with his mouth; that is a natural pain

Exercise can help prevent boredom and problem behaviors from occurring.

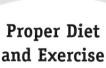

Proper Diet and Exercise

You may be looking at outside influences in trying to figure out why your Beagle acts a certain way when part of the problem may be internal. If your Beagle isn't getting a proper diet, this can affect his behavior. A vitamin deficiency, too much sugar or fatty foods, a medical prescription with certain side effects—all are diet-related contributors that can make your Beagle overly anxious, hyper, itchy and uncomfortable, and so on. Review the ingredient panel on the food you're giving him, and look closely at the other things he's ingesting.

Another contributor to boredom and anxiety is lack of exercise. It's something we as a society are guilty of. Our days tend to start too early, end too late, and be filled with all sorts of other obligations that squeeze out much-needed time for exercise. Young dogs especially need the right amount of exercise, but even seniors benefit from long walks. Every Beagle is different, and yours may need more exercise than others. Getting involved in a sport or activity (like those described in Chapter 8) may do both of you a world of good. Schedule it as you would one of your children's after-school activities. Take them along—they may want to get involved, too.

and shock reaction to a real hurt. Household aggression is defensive noncooperation or territoriality around possessions.

Solution

The best thing you can do for yourself, your family, and your Beagle is to call a professional right away. Aggression problems need to be treated properly and promptly so that they don't worsen. Qualified professionals include your veterinarian, who will need to assess if there's a physical source of pain that could be causing your Beagle to act out, and a trainer or behaviorist who has experience (and lots of references) working with aggressive dogs.

Barking

Beagles got their name because of their "loud mouths" (begeule in French), so you almost have to expect that you'll need to work on this one. Your friend simply may be unable to curb his enthusiasm, and so he

FAMILY-FRIENDLY TIP

Kids and Problem Behaviors

For children, self-control isn't always an option. When it comes to playing around dogs, this can sometimes cause tension and problems between species that should otherwise be the best of friends. Even the most trustworthy dog can "snap" if provoked badly enough or physically hurt, even if the injury wasn't intentional. Children who get used to hugging dogs occasionally may hug too hard. They may want to ride the Beagle by sitting on him and jabbing him with their legs. That's why it's so important for you to supervise play between your Beagle and your own and others' children. If you have any concerns, separate them. There's an old adage that goes "Once bitten, twice shy." A child who is suddenly turned on by an angry dog may never trust that dog again. The same is true for a dog who is suddenly mistreated by a child—he may never trust that child again.

expresses himself through his voice. Because those who love Beagles really do love their voices as well, allowing them to use them isn't the problem. It's allowing them to use them within reason that's desirable. How can you do that?

Solution

Dogs who like to bark can be taught to bark on cue, and once they know that you're asking them to bark, you then can teach them to "not bark," or shush, on cue. Working with your Beagle at a time when he likes to bark—when someone comes to the door, for example—set up the situation so that he will bark. When he does, cue the barking to a word like "speak," and enthusiastically sing along, saying "Good speak" and giving him a treat. When you've had enough, stop saying anything. Turn your back to your Beagle so that you aren't making eye contact. When he stops barking, turn around, say "Shush," and give him a treat. You will need to work on making this distinction clear for him, which could take time. One thing that won't work is trying to raise your voice to quiet him over his barking. If you don't like what he's doing, get something he's interested in, like treats, and only interact with him by feeding or praising him when he's doing what you want. Ignore all other behaviors.

Beagles who bark in their owners' absence are tough cases. Obviously, if you're not there, how can you work on the behavior? You likely will need to have a trainer come to your house to help while you're at work. It's a better solution than having your neighbors grow to hate you and your dogs.

Begging

Beagles are master beggars when allowed to practice the art. All it takes is one invitation from someone, like one of your children, your mother-in-law, or a dog-loving friend, for your Beagle to catch on that when he gives you his saddest, sweetest look while you're eating, there's something in it for him. Their size makes them small enough that they aren't really obnoxious, but their penetrating gaze is something that's hard to ignore and can disturb guests, even if it doesn't bother you.

Solution

If your Beagle already has a begging problem and won't be deterred from staring you down while you eat, you need to change his habits. The surest way to start is with confinement. Remove your Beagle from the dining room or kitchen while it's your dinnertime. Crate training

Beagles love to "talk"—it's part of their nature.

comes in handy for this because he should be happy enough to retreat to his crate, especially if there's an enticing chew toy in there for him. A baby gate can do the trick as long as he doesn't stand or pace at the gate, where he may develop another bad habit like drooling or barking at you. He should be somewhere where you can't make eye contact with each other. He may not like this at first and may protest by barking or whining. Stay resolute and don't give in. He'll eventually settle down.

Chasing

You could have a Beagle who becomes so crazy about squirrels that every time you open the door, he bolts out on a mission to chase down and capture any squirrels in the yard. Or when you walk him, he is on constant alert for movement, and when he sees

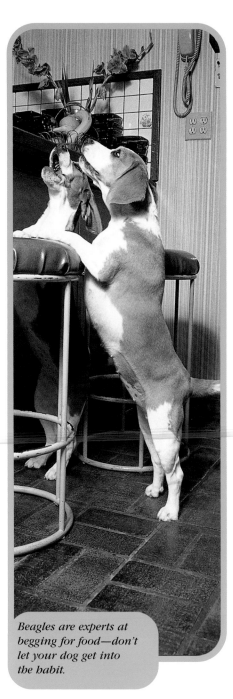

Beagles are experts at begging for food—don't let your dog get into the habit.

something, nearly drags you down the street, ignoring your pulling back or shouting.

Solution

Like barking, some of this instinct can't be trained out of a Beagle; it's who he is. You need to establish realistic expectations for yourself so that the behavior doesn't bother you as much. For example, if he's happily darting about the yard while you're inside, even if it's in winter when you want him to come in so that you can go to bed, you may need to just wait it out. Chances are if you don't go screaming or chasing after him, he'll decide it's nicer inside after all. If you're walking and he tends to jerk and pull you, explore walking him in a no-pull halter. Take treats on your walk so that he's more inclined to pay attention to you, not search for squirrels or cats.

Chewing

Whenever your Beagle finds and destroys something he's not supposed to, it's upsetting. If it's part of the furniture or a valuable keepsake, it's even more upsetting.

Solution

Your Beagle is probably bored. He also needs to be confined when he's not with you so that he doesn't have the opportunity to take and chew something he shouldn't. To help with the boredom, be sure that you're getting him out often

Professional Help

If your frustration level is building and your Beagle's behavior is deteriorating, it's time to seek professional help. Your veterinarian may be able to put you in touch with a trusted source, or you can find a trainer near you through the Association of Pet Dog Trainers (APDT) at 1-800-PET-DOGS or www.apdt.com.

enough. Is he home alone? Leaving a radio or TV on while you're gone will at least provide some white noise for him. While you have plenty to occupy your senses while you're out of the house, think of your poor dog lying there with nothing to do. No books, no movies, no crossword puzzles. He must have something appropriate to do. Interactive chew toys are popular for dogs in this

situation. There are all sorts of them these days, and a trip to a few pet stores to look at different varieties will be fun and very worthwhile. Help to make the toy irresistible to your Beagle by filling it with something sticky and stinky, like peanut butter, soft cheese, or small pieces of dog treats. You also should consider putting your Beagle in a doggy day care center or hiring a dog walker to visit with and take him out at least once while you're gone.

Digging

In his enthusiastic jaunts around the yard, does your Beagle like to stop and dig at the roses? Even when you catch him in the act and stop him, it doesn't seem to stop him.

Solution

If digging seems to be something your Beagle loves, why deny him? Instead, provide an area where he can dig to his heart's content. Designate a space big enough for him to enjoy, and put a

If your Beagle likes to dig, you might want to designate an area for this activity.

If Your Beagle Gets Lost

It's so true, and so scary. The fact is, it only takes a minute for your Beagle to become lost. Maybe you opened the front door when the phone rang, and in going to answer it didn't close the door properly. Your Beagle could wander out while you're on the phone. If you have a gated fenced-in yard, a forgetful child may not close the gate properly. For your Beagle, it's an opportunity to explore. With their curious natures and instinct to go sniffing, Beagles won't hesitate to explore the world, figuring you'll catch up to them.

The best way to defend against the loss of your Beagle is to be sure that he is properly identified. His well-fitted collar should sport an identification tag listing his name and your phone number(s). Because collars can come off wandering Beagles who get stuck in underbrush, a back-up identification method is advisable. Tattooing or microchipping are both options, although they are only as good as the ways they are registered so that someone can use them. When microchipped, you'll receive another tag for your dog's collar with a number to call. Most veterinary offices and animal shelters have scanners that can read microchips.

Should your Beagle become lost in your neighborhood, waste no time in making a flyer that you can distribute. It should include a clear picture of your Beagle showing as much of him as possible, the time, date, and location where he became lost, and several contact numbers. Distribute these to all the houses around you, as well as to the police, fire department, local veterinary offices, and animal shelters.

box around it so that it's like his own personal sand or dirt box. Fill it with loose dirt or sand, and praise him for digging there. If he still digs in spots where you don't want him to, reserve some of his feces and fill the holes with it. When he uncovers his own mess, he should be deterred.

House Soiling

Accidents will happen, but frequent accidents are a sign that your Beagle is not understanding what's expected of him, that you are not getting him out often enough, or even that you aren't thoroughly cleaning the sites of the accidents, so he wants to revisit them.

Solution

As reviewed in Chapter 6, effective housetraining requires a consistent schedule so that your Beagle gets out when he needs to. It also requires confinement to a crate or a room that's easy to clean up until he can be trusted unsupervised in other areas of the house. You also should ask your veterinarian if she suspects a medical condition that might make it hard for your Beagle to hold it.

If your veterinarian clears your Beagle, beyond paying closer attention to when he should need to go and where he is in the house, think about what might be causing his indiscretions. Does he soil when he gets upset about something, like sudden departures, social gatherings, or excessive noise? Is he

SENIOR DOG TIP

Helping an Older Dog Overcome Problems

Because problems are usually deep-rooted, it takes perception, understanding, and patience to try to unravel them. Fortunately, those who spend time doing this often write books about it, and if you go to your favorite book retailer and look for titles that address the problem you're having with your dog, you probably will find several worth reading. Older dogs with problems have had that much more time to fix them into their characters, and your road to "normal" may be a long one. Certainly you will need to learn all you can about what may be causing your dog's problem or problems, and you'll probably use a variety of methods to see what helps or doesn't. Patience is the key, and when you see your senior citizen coming around, you'll know it was all worth it.

91

revisiting the same spot? Consider having a professional cleaner come in to treat that area. Soiling in conjunction with other anxious behavior could be a sign of separation anxiety, and you should consult a professional.

Chapter 8

Stepping Out

If your Beagle is a typical happy-go-lucky fellow, you soon will discover that most outings turn into social outings. People can't seem to resist approaching and cooing over Beagles—and Beagles can't seem to resist the attention. This kind of positive experience gives strangers a great feeling about Beagles and gives Beagles a great feeling about strangers.

Common Courtesy

A wonderful thing about Beagles is that they're fairly nondiscriminating and are equally happy to greet neighbors, school kids, other dogs, and anyone else they come across. They will give strange people, and often, strange dogs, the benefit of the doubt and trust that if their experiences have been positive in the past, they will continue to be positive. Life teaches us that this isn't always the case. As the caretaker for your Beagle, and knowing what a magnet he is, it's important for you to have your antenna up when you are approached by strangers and strange dogs. If you sense that a quickly approaching dog is somewhat out of control and may not be trustworthy, cross the street or change directions. It would be a shame for your Beagle (or you) to be frightened or hurt by overly rowdy children or a snappy dog. Be mindful, too, of your own Beagle's manners. His enthusiasm to say hello may be interpreted by another dog as overly anxious, arousing a defensive response. Train your Beagle to greet people and other dogs calmly and respectfully.

Exploring the World With Your Beagle

Beagles are a great size to take everywhere with you. They're equally capable of spending a weekend hiking and camping as they are spending a weekend at a restful retreat. In fact, they are

SENIOR DOG TIP

Senior Travel Safety

Don't count your senior Beagle out just because you think he's slowing down. Truth is, he'll probably get more health benefits from tagging along than being left behind, which can be lonely and disconcerting. At the same time, don't take your senior's health for granted. Be sure to pack any prescription medications he'll need, the right amount of food, a special toy or blanket, a list of current medical concerns, extra materials for making him comfortable and cleaning up after him, and anything else you think will make him more comfortable. Be sensitive to the signals he's sending you, and try to give him the right amount of stimulation rather than too much or too little. Take pictures so that you can remember these good times.

happiest when they can be with you, so if your travel plans can accommodate your Beagle, bring him along.

Car Travel

A car will be your most frequent means of getting out and about, and your

Beagle should become used to car rides from puppyhood. Be sure to provide him a safe and secure spot, whether it's in a specially designed doggy seat belt or in a crate. The belt or the crate can keep your dog from becoming interested in an old french fry under the passenger seat or whatever else may distract him—and you—from the road.

The other things you'll need for your Beagle when traveling with him in the car include:

- A soft towel or blanket to sit on, whether on a seat or in his crate

- His collar with a full set of identification and health certification tags
- A sturdy leash
- A collapsible water bowl
- A basic first-aid kit
- Emergency medical information, including the name and phone number of your veterinarian, and any health problems your Beagle may have
- Enough of his regular food to get him through the time you'll be away (switching may upset his stomach, particularly if he's excited about traveling)
- Extra "doggy" towels for cleanups

Before you travel with your Beagle, make sure he is well-trained and well-socialized.

Even if it's just around the block, your Beagle loves to travel in style!

what requirements they have for the crate, check-in time, and so on. Rest assured that dogs fly frequently and that airlines take the responsibility of their safety seriously, but the better prepared you are for the trip, the more secure you'll feel.

Finding Pet-Friendly Lodgings

Knowing that you can take your Beagle almost anywhere with you doesn't mean that every hotel or motel will allow your Beagle in the building. To avoid any unpleasant surprises, make hotel or rental reservations well ahead of time and after receiving confirmation that your Beagle will be welcome. To start your search for pet-friendly places, find travel guides with listings, or search online. Because policies change frequently, don't trust that the information in a book is still accurate. Call or e-mail to confirm or ask questions.

When you stay at a pet-friendly place, don't be the one who convinces management that allowing dogs is a bad idea. Clean up after your dog, don't let him run amok in the room, be sure that he won't bark when you leave him alone, and respect the privacy of your neighbors. Remember, you're an ambassador for traveling with Beagles. You want to be welcomed wherever you go.

- Waste removal bags so that you can pick up after your dog when necessary

This list may seem excessive, but should you become involved in an accident, you don't want the fate of your Beagle left to chance. The more information you have about him in the car with you, the safer he'll be no matter what happens.

Planes

If you need to fly somewhere with your Beagle, make your plans well in advance of when you want to travel. Check the policies of every airline you're interested in to find out how your Beagle will travel in the plane and

Traveling With Your Beagle and Your Family

Packing the entire family into the car and heading off into the sunset can be exhilarating—and exhausting. When planning the trip, though, your Beagle may become overlooked when it comes to packing and preparing. Because he can't do much to help himself, other than get your attention somehow (not always in ways you want), you need to ask your children and spouse to shoulder some of the responsibility.

Sit down with your children, and if they're old enough, have them write out lists of the clothes they think they'll need or the special toys, games, or books they'll enjoy. Give them suggestions, complete the lists, and then ask them to do as much of the packing and organizing themselves as possible. For yourself, make a list of the things you'll need, and write down what you need to pack for your Beagle. If it makes life easier for you, designate a small suitcase for your Beagle's things. They'll be together in one place, and everyone will know where. When the final mad scramble comes, which it always does, you'll feel better if you know that everyone's bags are packed with what they want and need.

Getting Active With Your Beagle

There are so many things you and your Beagle could enjoy doing together that you might want to go beyond walks and get involved in an organized sport or other activity. You could explore the world of dog shows, obedience trials, agility, hunting, tracking, and even therapy visits to hospitals or nursing homes. You'll be surprised at what you and your Beagle can accomplish—and enjoy—together. An assortment of organizations that conduct these activities is listed in the Resources section.

Agility

This fun and fast-paced activity continues to be the fastest-growing dog sport in America. And no wonder—the action, the pace, the challenges, and the rewards all make it addicting to those who participate. Agility involves working your dog through an obstacle course where he is timed from start to finish and penalized for missing certain elements or going off-course. For whatever reasons, all dogs seem to take to

agility, even those who wouldn't normally be associated with something so fast and focused. If you want a really fun challenge, check it out.

Canine Good Citizen (CGC)

Your Beagle can actually earn a certificate from the American Kennel Club (AKC) for being a well-mannered member of society. If you go through basic training with your Beagle, learn about the CGC test and what your Beagle must do to pass it. The objective is to certify dogs who obey basic commands and who can handle the presence of friendly strangers and safe distractions. It's fun to say your Beagle

Agility is a fun, action-packed sport.

is a Canine Good Citizen, and earning this distinction promotes a positive image of the breed.

Conformation (Dog Shows)

In dog shows, people who are fanatical about their breed come together to compete with their dogs against others who are equally fanatical. To enjoy dog shows, you must want to bring out the absolute best in your Beagle and show him off to his peers and the world. It sounds like all you need is passion, but there is so much more to it. Before entering a show, go to several without your Beagle and observe and talk to people who are showing. If you think it's for you, work with a trustworthy breeder to acquire a show-potential puppy or dog. He will need to be intact (not neutered), and if you are bitten by the show bug, be prepared to become a true student of the Beagle.

Your Beagle's nose might win him a tracking title.

Hunting Tests and Field Trials

Back in the 1940s, being able to hunt with one or more Beagles for the simple sport of it is what made the breed so popular. Finding and tracking rabbits is, after all, what a Beagle is all about. Amazingly, even if you live in an apartment, you can find a group or a club that can help you get your Beagle into the field where he can really do his thing. What a gift for him and a thrill for you.

Hunting tests and field trials are organized by clubs who follow the rules of their breeds' registering bodies—the American Kennel Club (AKC) or United Kennel Club (UKC), for example. Hunting tests are designed to test and fine-tune basic instincts; field trials are for Beaglers who are very serious about hunting. If this interests you, don't be intimidated. Find a club near you, and attend an event or two to watch and meet others, and to learn more about this time-honored sport.

The Expert Knows

Sports and Safety

When you discover any one of the multiple ways you can become more active with your Beagle, you may be tempted to do it all and do it now. As you introduce your Beagle to new experiences, be mindful of his overall appearance and energy level, which will give you clues about how he's accepting everything. If you push too hard too fast, you may stress your Beagle. This could manifest itself through itching, overexcitement, irregular appetite, or other aberrant behavior. Remember the story of the tortoise and the hare: Slow and steady wins the race.

Obedience Trials

These are formal competitions in which dog-handler teams are judged on the precision and accuracy of completing specific commands, from walking at different speeds off lead to scent discrimination and retrieving. Beagles are often generalized as being too "stubborn" or "independent" to do well at obedience, but many have defied those generalizations and gone on to earn titles. If the training bug takes you in this direction with your Beagle, go for it and see how many people you'll amaze.

Therapy Work

With the right temperament and some basic training, your Beagle could be on his way to brightening the lives of many who no longer have dogs of their own because they are in care facilities or hospitals. Children and older people are the frequent recipients of pet therapy visits, and the difference pets make for these folks is well documented. The Delta Society, Therapy Dogs International (TDI), and Therapy Dogs Incorporated are all national organizations that can help to get you started.

Tracking

With their exceptional sense of smell, Beagles are natural trackers. Tracking is a sport that was organized to test a dog's ability to find and stay on a scent. Trails are made hours ahead of time, and competing dog-handler teams go out "cold" on them, starting at a marked pole and ending when their dog finds the scented glove. Judges who know the lines assess how well the dogs do. Tracking training is its own kind of addiction, and watching your Beagle use his nose this way can be extremely rewarding.

Is Your Beagle a Show Dog?

If you're like so many of us who have fallen head-over-heels for your breed, you may feel like you want to show the world how wonderful your special Beagle is. In your opinion, the fine fellow who worships the ground you walk on is certainly better looking than the Beagles you see in the dog shows on TV, right? You imagine your Beagle being awarded a blue ribbon—the ultimate proof for your belief that he is the very best. You watch some dog shows on TV and begin to learn more about showing dogs through your Beagle's devout breeder. Or maybe one of your kids thinks showing your Beagle would be fun. But how do you know if your Beagle has the right stuff? How do you determine if he's as gorgeous as you think—and how do you get involved in showing?

Remember, Beagles are one of the most popular breeds, so there are a lot of them in the world. The larger their numbers, the harder it is to have a truly outstanding Beagle (for the show ring— don't take that personally!). People who are serious about showing and breeding dogs want to be sure they're not wasting their time or money before they step into the show ring. They study the Beagle's written standard to understand his form and function. They have a picture of the "perfect" Beagle in their head: the length of his ears, the shape

of his eyes, the length of his back, how he holds his tail, his coloring, and so much more. Dog-show people become devotees of their breeds, quickly summing up any "faults" (things that don't look good) so they can assess a puppy's potential for the show ring.

If you're serious about this stuff, too, you want to make friends with people who have been studying Beagles for a long time. Go to shows and watch the Beagle judging. Catch up with the people who are showing the winning dogs. They may own them, or they may simply be showing (handling) them for someone else. Whether owner or handler, politely ask if he or she can tell you about their dog—what sets him apart, what makes him one of the winners.

As you're learning about Beagles who are already show dogs, bring your perspective home. Read the standard for the Beagle. Start looking carefully at your dog. If you still like what you see, ask your breeder for his or her opinion. If the feedback is positive, you'll need to take your passion to the next level and start seriously studying how to groom and handle your Beagle for the show ring. The friends you've met and made through your observations and discussions should be happy to help.

Resources

Associations and Organizations

Breed Clubs

American Kennel Club (AKC)
5580 Centerview Drive
Raleigh, NC 27606
Telephone: (919) 233-9767
Fax: (919) 233-3627
E-mail: info@akc.org
www.akc.org

Canadian Kennel Club (CKC)
89 Skyway Avenue, Suite 100
Etobicoke, Ontario M9W 6R4
Telephone: (416) 675-5511
Fax: (416) 675-6506
E-mail: information@ckc.ca
www.ckc.ca

Federation Cynologique Internationale (FCI)
Secretariat General de la FCI
Place Albert 1er, 13
B – 6530 Thuin
Belqique
www.fci.be

The Kennel Club
1 Clarges Street
London
W1J 8AB
Telephone: 0870 606 6750
Fax: 0207 518 1058
www.the-kennel-club.org.uk

United Kennel Club (UKC)
100 E. Kilgore Road
Kalamazoo, MI 49002-5584
Telephone: (269) 343-9020
Fax: (269) 343-7037
E-mail: pbickell@ukcdogs.com
www.ukcdogs.com

Pet Sitters

National Association of Professional Pet Sitters
15000 Commerce Parkway, Suite C
Mt. Laurel, New Jersey 08054
Telephone: (856) 439-0324
Fax: (856) 439-0525
E-mail: napps@ahint.com
www.petsitters.org

Pet Sitters International
201 East King Street
King, NC 27021-9161
Telephone: (336) 983-9222
Fax: (336) 983-5266
E-mail: info@petsit.com
www.petsit.com

Rescue Organizations and Animal Welfare Groups

American Humane Association (AHA)
63 Inverness Drive East
Englewood, CO 80112
Telephone: (303) 792-9900
Fax: 792-5333
www.americanhumane.org

American Society for the
Prevention of Cruelty to Animals
(ASPCA)
424 E. 92nd Street
New York, NY 10128-6804
Telephone: (212) 876-7700
www.aspca.org

Royal Society for the Prevention of
Cruelty to Animals (RSPCA)
Telephone: 0870 3335 999
Fax: 0870 7530 284
www.rspca.org.uk

The Humane Society of the United
States (HSUS)
2100 L Street, NW
Washington DC 20037
Telephone: (202) 452-1100
www.hsus.org

Sports

International Agility Link (IAL)
Global Administrator: Steve Drinkwater
E-mail: yunde@powerup.au
www.agilityclick.com/~ial

North American Dog Agility
Council
11522 South Hwy 3
Cataldo, ID 83810
www.nadac.com

United States Dog Agility
Association
P.O. Box 850955
Richardson, TX 75085-0955
Telephone: (972) 487-2200
www.usdaa.com

Therapy

Delta Society
875 124th Ave NE, Suite 101
Bellevue, WA 98005
Telephone: (425) 226-7357
Fax: (425) 235-1076
E-mail: info@deltasociety.org
www.deltasociety.org

Therapy Dogs Incorporated
PO Box 5868
Cheyenne, WY 82003
Telephone: (877) 843-7364
E-mail: therdog@sisna.com
www.therapydogs.com

Therapy Dogs International (TDI)
88 Bartley Road
Flanders, NJ 07836
Telephone: (973) 252-9800
Fax: (973) 252-7171
E-mail: tdi@gti.net
www.tdi-dog.org

Training

Association of Pet Dog Trainers
(APDT)
150 Executive Center Drive Box 35
Greenville, SC 29615
Telephone: (800) PET-DOGS
Fax: (864) 331-0767
E-mail: information@apdt.com
www.apdt.com

National Association of Dog
Obedience Instructors (NADOI)
PMB 369
729 Grapevine Hwy.
Hurst, TX 76054-2085
www.nadoi.org

Veterinary and Health Resources

Academy of Veterinary Homeopathy (AVH)
P.O. Box 9280
Wilmington, DE 19809
Telephone: (866) 652-1590
Fax: (866) 652-1590
E-mail: office@TheAVH.org
www.theavh.org

American Academy of Veterinary Acupuncture (AAVA)
100 Roscommon Drive, Suite 320
Middletown, CT 06457
Telephone: (860) 635-6300
Fax: (860) 635-6400
E-mail: office@aava.org
www.aava.org

American Animal Hospital Association (AAHA)
P.O. Box 150899
Denver, CO 80215-0899
Telephone: (303) 986-2800
Fax: (303) 986-1700
E-mail: info@aahanet.org
www.aahanet.org/index.cfm

American College of Veterinary Internal Medicine (ACVIM)
1997 Wadsworth Blvd., Suite A
Lakewood, CO 80214-5293
Telephone: (800) 245-9081
Fax: (303) 231-0880
E-mail: ACVIM@ACVIM.org
www.acvim.org

American College of Veterinary Ophthalmologists (ACVO)
P.O. Box 1311
Meridian, Idaho 83860
Telephone: (208) 466-7624
Fax: (208) 466-7693
E-mail: office@acvo.com
www.acvo.com

American Holistic Veterinary Medical Association (AHVMA)
2218 Old Emmorton Road
Bel Air, MD 21015
Telephone: (410) 569-0795
Fax: (410) 569-2346
E-mail: office@ahvma.org
www.ahvma.org

American Veterinary Medical Association (AVMA)
1931 North Meacham Road – Suite 100
Schaumburg, IL 60173
Telephone: (847) 925-8070
Fax: (847) 925-1329
E-mail: avmainfo@avma.org
www.avma.org

ASPCA Animal Poison Control Center
1717 South Philo Road, Suite 36
Urbana, IL 61802
Telephone: (888) 426-4435
www.aspca.org

British Veterinary Association (BVA)
7 Mansfield Street
London
W1G 9NQ
Telephone: 020 7636 6541
Fax: 020 7436 2970
E-mail: bvahq@bva.co.uk
www.bva.co.uk

Canine Eye Registration Foundation
(CERF)
VMDB/CERF
1248 Lynn Hall
625 Harrison St.
Purdue University
West Lafayette, IN 47907-2026
Telephone: (765) 494-8179
E-mail: CERF@vmbd.org
www.vmdb.org

Orthopedic Foundation for
Animals (OFA)
2300 NE Nifong Blvd
Columbus, Missouri 65201-3856
Telephone: (573) 442-0418
Fax: (573) 875-5073
E-mail: ofa@offa.org
www.offa.org

Publications

Books

Anderson, Teoti. *The Super Simple Guide to Housetraining*. Neptune City, NJ: TFH Publications, 2004.

De Vito, Dominique. *Animal Planet® Pet Care Library: Training Your Dog*. Neptune City, NJ: TFH Publications, 2007.

Goldstein, Robert J., VMD, and Susan. *The Goldsteins' Wellness & Longevity Program for Dogs and Cats*. Neptune City, NJ: TFH Publications, 2005.

King, Trish. *Parenting Your Dog*. Neptune City, NJ: TFH Publications, 2004.

McCullough, Susan. *Beagles for Dummies*. Hoboken, NJ: For Dummies, 2006.

Morgan, Diane. *Good Dogkeeping*. Neptune City, NJ: TFH Publications, 2005.

Silvani, Pia and Lynn Eckhardt. *Raising Puppies and Kids Together: A Guide for Parents*. Neptune City, NJ: TFH Publications, 2005.

Yin, Sophia, DVM. *How to Behave So Your Dog Behaves*. Neptune City, NJ: TFH Publications, 2004.

Magazines

AKC *Family Dog*
American Kennel Club
260 Madison Avenue
New York, NY 10016
Telephone: (800) 490-5675
E-mail: familydog@akc.org
www.akc.org/pubs/familydog

AKC *Gazette*
American Kennel Club
260 Madison Avenue
New York, NY 10016
Telephone: (800) 533-7323
E-mail: gazette@akc.org
www.akc.org/pubs/gazette

The American Beagler
P.O. Box 39327
Indianapolis, IN 46239
Telephone: (317) 356-3303
www.geocities.com/ctailblues/aba.html

Beagles Unlimited
A magazine and website devoted to maintaining the hunting instincts of the Beagle.
Donald J. Potts, Webmaster and Editor
www.beaglesunlimited.net

Better Beagling
P.O. Box 8142
Essex, VT 05451
Telephone: (802) 878-3616
www.betrbeagle.com

Dog & Kennel
Pet Publishing, Inc.
7-L Dundas Circle
Greensboro, NC 27407
Telephone: (336) 292-4272
Fax: (336) 292-4272
E-mail: info@petpublishing.com
www.dogandkennel.com

Dog Fancy
Subscription Department
P.O. Box 53264
Boulder, CO 80322-3264
Telephone: (800) 365-4421
E-mail: barkback@dogfancy.com
www.dogfancy.com

Dogs Monthly
Ascot House
High Street, Ascot,
Berkshire SL5 7JG
United Kingdom
Telephone: 0870 730 8433
Fax: 0870 730 8431
E-mail: admin@rtc-associates.freeserve.co.uk
www.corsini.co.uk/dogsmonthly

Hounds & Hunting Magazine
P.O. Box 372
Bradford, PA 16701
Telephone: (814) 368-6154 or 6155
www.houndsandhunting.com

Websites

Nylabone
1 TFH Plaza
3rd & Union Avenues
Neptune, NJ 07753
Telephone: (800) 631-2188
E-mail: info@nylabone.com
www.nylabobe.com

107

Index

annual examination, 54
cleaning, 46, 46
ear mites, 64
grooming, 43
infections of, 46, 67-68
Edward III, King, 7
Elizabeth I, Queen, 7
emergencies
first aid, 65
lost pets, 90
staying calm, 66
encephalitis, 66
energy levels, 15, 34
epilepsy, 59
Evert, Chris, 7
examination, annual, 54-56
exercise
behavior problems and,
84, 85
recommendations, 15
scheduling, 24
X-pen, 24-25
external parasites, 55, 63-66
eye contact, 78
eyes
aging and, 9
annual examination, 54
cleaning, 45-46
glaucoma, 59
grooming, 43, 47

F
famous owners, 7
fats, 29
Fedération Cynologique
International (FCI), 10,
103
feeding Beagles
amounts of food, 35-36
begging for food, 39,
87-88, 88
behavior problems and, 85
children and, 29
commercial dog food,
30-33
feeding times, 34-35
free-feeding, 35
home-cooked diet, 32-34
leftovers, 39
love of food, 13
noncommercial foods,
32-34
nutritional standards,
29-31
obesity and, 36-37
overview, 28
preservatives in food, 32

prohibited foods, 31
raw diet, 32
supplies, 22-24
table manners, 37-39
feet, examining, 56
fertilizers, 67
field trials, 10, 99
first aid
for accidents, 66-67
kit contents, 65
for poisoning, 68-69
removing ticks, 66
fleas, 62-64
food bowls, 22-23
form and function, 11
Foxhounds, 7-8
free-feeding, 35

G
Gabor, Eva, 7
glaucoma, 59
grapes, 31
grooming
areas needing attention,
42
bathing dogs, 47-48
benefits of, 42
brushing dogs, 45
dental care, 48, 48-49
drying dogs, 48
ears, 46, 46, 67
eyes, 45-46
selecting location, 44
supplies for, 24, 42-44
tables for, 44-45
trimming nails, 44, 46-47
grooming tables, 44-45
gums. See dental
considerations

H
Hamilton, George, 7
Harriers, 8, 10
health considerations. See
also illnesses/diseases
accidents, 66-67
aching joints, 9, 33
allergies, 67
alternative therapies, 69
annual examination,
54-56
breeding and, 60
DHLPP shot and, 57-58
diarrhea, 67
ear infections, 46, 67-68
external parasites, 55,
63-66

finding a veterinarian,
52-54
grooming as health check,
43
hot spots, 68
internal parasites, 61-63
nutritional diet and, 28
poisoning, 31, 67-69
for senior dogs, 53
taking dog's temperature,
62
vaccinations, 56-59
vomiting, 69
heart and lungs
annual examination, 55
heart murmurs, 59-60
heartworm, 61
pulmonic stenosis, 60
heart murmurs, 59-60
heartworm, 61
Heaton, Patricia, 7
heel command, 75, 80-81
hepatitis, 57
herbal therapy, 69
Herriott, James, 7
history of Beagles, 6-7
home-cooked diet, 32-34
homeopathy, 69
hookworm, 61
hound glove, 42
house soiling, 90-91
housetraining
crates during, 73-74
feeding considerations
when, 34-35
house soiling and, 90-91
responding to accidents,
74-75
supplies for, 25
hunting
activities for, 99
Beagles and, 7-10, 15
tapeworms from, 62
ticks from, 64

I
ID tags, 21, 90
illnesses/diseases
alternative therapies, 69
cherry eye, 59
DHLPP shot and, 57-58
dilated cardiomyopathy,
60
distemper, 57
encephalitis, 66
epilepsy, 59
eye and ear discharges, 54

111

Dedication

This book is dedicated to all those who rescue and care for the many Beagles who need new and forever families. You are the Beagles' true Heroes.

About the Author

Dominique De Vito has been involved in pet publishing for over 10 years, and has helped create many award-winning books. A member of the Association of Pet Dog Trainers and the Dog Writers Association of America, she is the author of *Training Your Dog* for the Animal Planet™ Pet Care Library. She is currently a freelance editor and writer who lives with her husband, three dogs, and twin boys in New Jersey and New York state.

Photo Credits

Theresa Martinez (Shutterstock): 4
verityjohnson (Shutterstock): 16
Tad Denson (Shutterstock): 21
Gregg Cerenzio (Shutterstock): 26, 70
Michael Borders (Shutterstock): 40
Jack S (Shutterstock): 50
Rhonda Odonnell (Shutterstock): 82
anyka (Shutterstock): 92
All other photos courtesy of Isabelle Francais and TFH archives.
Cover photo: Isabelle Francais

REACH OUT. ACT. RESPOND.

Go to AnimalPlanet.com/ROAR and find out how you can be a voice for animals everywhere!